Holy Spirit Power

Can Change The World

By Bob Williams

Foreword By
Rev. Msgr. Anthony M. Tocco

Introduction By
James "Butch" Murphy

Holy Spirit Power Press, Bloomfield Hills, MI

II

Nihil obstat: **Rev. Robert J. McClory**
Censor Deputatus
August 11, 2003

Imprimatur: **†Adam Cardinal Maida**
Archbishop of Detroit
August 11, 2003
Feast of St. Clare of Assisi

ISBN 0-9743115-0-2

Library of Congress Control Number 2003110765

Printed in the United States by Data Reproductions, Corporation

Dedication

This book, my first, is dedicated to my wife Sue who has put up with years of me being in the basement at my computer. She would call down, "What you doing?" and I would respond, "Working on my book". Keep in mind that this has been going on since 1992 when I first started writing articles for the St. Hugo's Herald which are the foundation for this book. Very important is Sue's skill as a proof reader, she can literally find a "needle in a hay stack" and she did many times. Thanks Sue for being my top notch proof reader. What ever graces the Lord might bestow because of this book, I ask Him to bestow them on you.

HOLY SPIRIT POWER

IS THE ONLY

POWER STRONG ENOUGH

TO OVERCOME

THE EVIL

IN OUR WORLD

Jesus tells us in Luke 10:19
"Behold, I have given you the power 'to tread upon
serpents' and scorpions and upon the full force
of the enemy and nothing will harm you."

Content

VIII

Foreword

Bob's book is about one of the ancient beliefs of the Church. It calls us to understand the Charismatic Dimension of our faith and to know better the supernatural gifts of the Spirit referred to as Charisms.

In the documents of Vatican II, this Charismatic Dimension of the Church is written about seven times in four of the Council documents:
:

• Dogmatic Constitution On The Church

• Decree On The Ministry And Life of Priest

• Decree On The Apostolate Of Lay People

• Decree On The Church's Missionary Activity

In these references the charisms are related to St. Paul's First Letter to the Corinthians 12. The Holy Spirit is written about two hundred and fifty times in the sixteen documents.

Bob's thesis is that this power of the Holy Spirit through His Charisms, that Jesus promised us in Luke 10:19, Luke 24:49 and Acts of the Apostles 1:8, is needed if we are going to restore a world that is literally falling apart morally, to the peace and love Jesus intended for it.

He suggests that it is time for Church authorities to take up the subject of the Charismatic Dimension of the Church as presented by the Vatican II Documents; study them and start implementing them into the life of the Church as other documents were.

He also makes it clear that he is not just talking about the Charismatic Renewal with its prayer meetings, praying in tongues, raising of hands, personal growth of its membership and very exuberant singing. He points out that these are certainly part of the Charismatic Dimension of the Church but are not its essence.

The essence of this Charismatic Dimension of the Church is the Power of the Holy Spirit as expressed through the supernatural gifts, the Charisms. This Power of the Spirit is meant for all members of the Body of Christ, the Church, and should be understood and accepted by them.

I agree with Bob's thesis and challenge readers of this book to consider it seriously and follow up on his suggestions.

Cheers in the Lord,
Rev. Monsignor Anthony M. Tocco
Pastor, St. Hugo of the Hills
Parish Community*

*St. Hugo's is in the Archdiocese of Detroit. It has 3,900 families, a K-8 school with 850 students and 500 children in its Religious Education Program. It is known for its charities, community service, youth ministry and adult education. Liturgies are Spirit filled with a high level of participation in song and prayer. Homilies are attention getting, based on scripture, motivational, and action oriented toward carrying out the mission of Jesus.

Acknowledgements

- My parents, Bill and Bessie Williams, for their love, solid Christian example, and challenge to do my best. My brothers; George, Arthur, Roger, and William; who were great companions and supported me in my endeavors. I am sure that Mom, Dad and my brothers are cheering for me from their heavenly home that this book will be a success.

- Elizabeth Williams, my daughter, who was instrumental in getting me involved in the Catholic Charismatic Renewal.

- Bill Williams, my son, who coached me in how to better use my computer and the internet. He designed the cover page.

- Father John Hampsch, C.M.F. who conducted the mini Life In The Spirit Seminar at the Silverdome on July 30, 1988.

- Three people on the program at the July 1988 Charismatic Conference, who really impressed and influenced me:
  - Jim "Butch" Murphy my prime educator in the "Spirit".
  - Bob Olson from the Upper Peninsula, a prime motivator.
  - Father Art Cooney, OFM Cap. a very charismatic priest.

- John & Jane Hanzel, for their example and spirituality.

- Sister Lucille Smalley, IHM a sounding board and advisor.

- All members of The Light Of God Prayer Group.

- All members of the Detroit and Michigan Charismatic Renewal Centers, especially Arlene Apone, Mary Ann Przybysz, Darlene Czop, Rosemary Marsal. Patty Stamford, and Paul Marciniak.

- John Siler, a dear friend, Christian model, confidant, and educator who moved to his home in heaven October 26, 2002.

- Blessed Pope John XXIII for his contribution to the Church, Vatican II, and his prayer, "O Holy Spirit, renew your wonders in this our day as a new Pentecost."

- Léon Joseph Cardinal Suenens who was responsible for getting reference to the charisms included in the Vatican II documents and his book, "A New Pentecost."

- Fathers Killian McDonnsll, O.S.B. and George Montague, S.M. authors of "Christian Initiation and Baptism In The Holy Spirit, Evidence From The First Eight Centuries." This book convinced me that the Catholic Church was a fully Charismatic Church from the very start, that much of this dimension was lost, and has never been fully restored even after Vatican II.

- St. Hugo of the Hills Parish Community priests:
Msgr. Tony Tocco my inspiring pastor for eighteen years.
Associates: Jim Rafferty, Joseph Szewczyk, Bob Schuster, Jim Beloit, Jack Baker, Nick Zukowski and Ron Essman.
Week End Associates: Mike Buentello, John Zenz, George Hazler.

- Katie Dailey for her review of the book's content and suggestions for improvement.

- Trudy Mohan, Mary Russell, and Donna Stenwall for their comments and suggestions.

- Finally, but most important, the Holy Spirit who gave me the power to learn about Him, love Him and write about Him.

Introduction

Bob Williams would not make a good politician. He's too honest, too direct!!

In his typical "here it is" style, Bob lays out for us a compelling case to reconsider and take seriously the role of the Holy Spirit in the Church today.

Bob, I believe, makes two basic points in this book:

- The Church is struggling to achieve its mission.

- The power of the Holy Spirit is lacking and is needed in the Church today.

At first glance the problem and solution might seem simplistic.

Upon further study and reflection, however, one comes to realize that the grace of the Holy Spirit is more profound and challenging than the mere sentimental nod to a white dove painted on a banner in the church sanctuary.

Bob portrays the Holy Spirit as anything but calm and passive. Williams rather, with solid references, shows the action of the Holy Spirit to be energetic, dynamic and challenging. He goes on to point out that this same Spirit seeks to make us this same way, people who ignite the Spirit's power in them.

The author argues that, for the Church to be authentic it must both acknowledge and embrace the charismatic dimension of the Church, a Church founded by Jesus…upon the apostles…for a dynamic global mission: the salvation of the Human race.

Bob, I believe makes a compelling case for just such a reclamation of this vibrancy of the Spirit's power.

As Williams presses the point, you may be tempted to see the book as an interesting concept for armchair theologians, but of no real value to the average Catholic.

This is precisely for the average Catholic....so that they may be average no longer, but operate with the power of the Holy Spirit as Jesus promised us.

The power Bob describes can absolutely revolutionize one's life, one's family, one's job and one's world.

I urge you to commit to having an open mind and seriously consider the thesis presented.

After the end of your reading, there is one question I think you must honestly address;

IS BOB WILLIAMS RIGHT OR IS HE WRONG?
I and several million others say he is right.

May the Holy Spirit Himself guide you with His knowledge, wisdom and discernment as you wrestle with this same question.

James "Butch" Murphy, President
Vera Cruz Communications*

*Vera Cruz [True Cross] Communications exists to proclaim the message of God's love, evidenced by the cross of Jesus. The core of its message is a belief that this vital message must be presented in ways that are understandable, not only to Christians, but to secular listeners. Its mission is achieved by Training Programs, Seminars, Consultations, Coaching and Speaking Engagements.

Abbreviations

AA   Apostolican Actvositaten, Decree On The Apostilate of Lay People

CCC   Catechism of the Catholic Church

Divi   Dominum et Vivificanten, On The Holy Spirit In The Life Of The Church And The World

GS   Gaudium et spes, Pastoral Constitution On The Church In The Modern World

LG   Lumen Gentium, Dogmatic Constitution On The Church

PO   Presbyterorum ordinis, Decree On The Ministry And Life Of Priests

RM   Redemptoris Missio, Mission Of The Redeemer

Prayer For Guidance

Pope John Paul II in his general Audience of May 17, 1989 said this about the Holy Spirit:

"Thus the Paraclete, the Holy Spirit of Truth, is man's true Counselor."

Each time you read from this book, ask the Holy Spirit to be your Spirit of Truth and Counselor. Say this prayer:

HOLY SPIRIT, THIRD PERSON

OF THE BLESSED TRINITY,

AS I READ THIS BOOK

I ASK YOU TO BE MY SPIRIT

OF TRUTH AND MY COUNSELOR,

OPEN MY HEART AND MIND

TO HAVE A CORRECT UNDERSTANDING

OF YOU AND YOUR GIFTS TO ME

AND THE CHURCH. AMEN

Chapter 1

Why This Book At This Time?

Introduction

The story of my growth as a Christian is the story of how this book came about. It is the story of how God had a plan for my life and would not let go of me until I sensed what it was and accepted its challenge. He then turned me over to the Holy Spirit so I would have His power to carry out God's work assigned to me.

It is my intention in this chapter to give you some of the main events in my life that were engineered by the Holy Spirit that led to my writing this book on the Charismatic Dimension of the Catholic Church. I was convinced that the Power of the Holy Spirit needed to be better known, understood, and used. The power promised to us by Jesus so we as individuals and the Church can live and act to achieve the mission God has for His people.

My Early Years

It all started October 17, 1919, when I was born to Bill and Bessie Williams, the second of five boys; George, Robert, Arthur, Roger and William. Dad was a Medical Doctor and Mom a Registered Nurse. We were a close knit family and most of the activities we were involved in were as a family. My formal religious education was limited, through 8th grade of the Baltimore Catechism. My parents, through their excellent example as Catholics, gave me a practical religious education. The five of us graduated from Whitesboro, New York High School.

After graduating from Syracuse University in May 1943, I spent 4 years in the Navy where I met Suzanne B. Leferovich. We were

2

married February 15, 1947 at St. Michael's Church in Syracuse, NY. We have two children: Bill, who lives in Texas and has three children and Elizabeth, who lives in Detroit and has two children. An event that would play a role later in my life was taking the Dale Carnegie Course, continuing with Instructor Training and teaching the course for five years.

My first job in accounting with a Syracuse firm started me on a path of advancement. After 10 years, I decided it was time to make a change and accepted a job in Cranston, RI with a major company as Controller. The *first* significant action of the Holy Spirit in my life occurred after I had been on this new job for only 9 months. I received a phone call from my former boss telling me the company was moving to Detroit and merging with another company. He was offered the job of Controller for these merged companies but turned it down because he did not want to move. I was offered the job, accepted, and started in February 1958.

Life In Michigan

While getting settled in this new job the *second* significant action of the Holy Spirit in my life took place. It was a Sunday and I was in the suburbs of Detroit house hunting so I could move my family here. Earlier that morning I went to Mass but could not receive communion because of the fasting regulations in effect at that time. Around noon I passed by St. Bede Church in Southfield, Michigan with many cars in the parking lot indicating Mass was in progress. As my fast time was over I stopped, received communion, picked up a bulletin, and went on my way. That evening back at the hotel this is what I read in the bulletin: "Gain Self Confidence and Poise, Speak Effectively, and Put Purpose In Your Life. Call Father Bresnahan for more information." As a Dale Carnegie Instructor all I could think is, "what in the world is the Catholic Church up to now?" Monday morning I called Father Bresnahan and this started me on a 16 year adventure with the Gabriel Richard Institute, 6 as a volunteer and 10 as Associate Director. This started me on the road from being just a "Sunday Go

To Mass Catholic" to making my faith part of me 7 days a week. This also developed in me a bunch of new skills; developing training manuals, writing these manuals, developing and conducting a problem solving course for Nuns and Brothers to help them cope with the effect of Vatican II on their lives.

In 1973, I resigned from the Gabriel Richard Institute as Associate Director. This lead me on a path to further development of my knowledge and skills as General Manager of a small publishing company for five years and for ten years as Consultant for a personnel search firm. I retired in 1988 only to come out of retirement in 1992 to be Business Manager of my parish, St. Hugo of the Hills. This was a parish of 3,500 families, an 850 student school and a budget of over $3 million. This introduced me to how a large parish operates and its relationship to the diocese. I made a real contribution by updating their accounting and reporting systems and reorganizing its maintenance department. It became apparent a stronger computer and construction background was needed so I resigned in April 1995 when a new person was hired. My real enjoyment and growth was in working with the Pastor, Msgr. Tocco, the Associate Pastors, the office staff, and the many highly qualified parishioners who made up the many commissions and committees of this very active parish.

The Charismatic Renewal

In 1988, the *third* significant action of the Holy Spirit on my life took place and was a motivator to writing this book. Elizabeth, our daughter, came to me with a problem. The Michigan Charismatic Renewal was holding their conference at the Silverdome in Pontiac on July 29-31, 1988. Space had been reserved at Pontiac Catholic for the Youth Events but was, at the last minute, cancelled because of needed repairs. Elizabeth asked me if I would contact the Prayer Group Leadership to find out if the youth could use St. Hugo's School. After some investigation and a few phone calls, I got in contact with Jane Hanzel who was on the Pastoral Team for the Light of God Prayer Group. Within 24

4

hours, space at St. Hugo's School was approved by Sister Margaret, School Principal. Elizabeth gave us a copy of the conference schedule and asked if we would like to go. The only thing on the schedule that looked Catholic was the Sunday Mass so we agreed to go. We live just 5 miles south of the Silverdom so Elizabeth and a friend of hers, Darlene Czop, stayed at our house. When they returned Friday evening, Darlene asked if we were going Saturday, we responded that we would go to the Sunday Mass. Next thing we knew, they were praying over us and at times using some strange language. At 8:30 AM Saturday we were at the Sivlerdome.

This gave the Holy Spirit a *fourth* opportunity to exert His influence on me. That afternoon Father John Hampsch, C.M.F. conducted a mini Life In The Spirit Seminar. In 2 hours he gave what usually takes 14 hours; it was effective. For the first time I heard, or at least understood, how much God loved me by sending his Son to die on the cross for me and how much Jesus wanted to have a personal relationship with me. Father explained about the charisms, gifts of the Holy Spirit, and how the Father and the Son wanted us to have these gifts so we would have the power to live the life They had planned for us. My reaction was, "this is great!" Why was I, 67, before learning about and understanding all these great things about the Catholic Faith? I vowed I would do something so this would not happen to others.

Incident *five*, the Holy Spirit used a paint brush to introduce me to the Charismatic Dimension of the Catholic Church. Sue and I regularly attended the Light of God Prayer Meetings. At one meeting, a plea was made for volunteers to help paint their new headquarters space at Martyrs of Uganda Convent in Detroit. I volunteered. After a day of painting as I was leaving the office a fine looking bearded man came up to me and said he would open the parking lot gate for me. It turned out that this was Jim "Butch" Murphy, Director of the Detroit Renewal Center, became Director of the Michigan Renewal Center then a member of the National Service Committee. Butch and I became close friends and I was privileged to work with him on many occasions both on a Detroit and State level. This gave me an in-depth introduction to the Charismatic Renewal and what the Charismatic Dimension of the Church could mean in terms of achieving the mission Jesus gave His Church. The Holy Spirit was really tugging on me to get deeper into this dimension of the Church.

I became very involved in the Light of God Prayer Group at St. Hugo's and soon became a member of its Pastoral Team. I was asked to take the responsibility for supplying articles for the Prayer Group's column in St. Hugo's bulletin. This was a simple matter of reading, selecting, and giving articles to the bulletin editor. Then the Holy Spirit stepped into my life for the *sixth* time. A decision was made that for all articles we needed written permission to use. This was an impossible task for me because of the time involved. The Spirit then spoke to me saying "you are to write articles for the Herald yourself". I really balked at this because I had no writing experience but it was either this or give up the column. In 1992, I started out with a pad, pencil, and old L.C. Smith typewriter and Sue as my proof reader. Now I have a computer with Word and Spell Check and about 300 reference books purchased and read over the years. I have written over 400 articles for the Herald. This experience educated me in the Catholic Faith, especially its Charismatic Dimension. This experience convinced me that the Charismatic Dimension of the Church must be restored. I was convicted by the Spirit to write a book about Him and the power He can give the Church and to members of the Body of Christ through His charisms.

The Holy Spirit set me up six times so I could clearly understand God's plan for me; He will do the same for you. By living it you will have excitement and reward in your life. He will not send you an e-mail nor an express mail but He will talk to you through the Holy Spirit. Jesus ends His parable of the sower, Luke 8:8b. "Whoever has ears to hear ought to hear." Be quiet and listen for the Spirit's whisper of discernment, knowledge, and wisdom.

Your Thoughts and Ideas:

- What has the Spirit done for me?
- What do you want the Spirit to do for you?
- What do you want to get out of this book?
- Ideas that come to you as you read.

Chapter 2

After 2000 Years, Where Do We Stand?

Jesus' Instructions To Us

We can evaluate where the Church stands today only by having a bench mark for comparison. Jesus gave us this bench mark. These are the words Jesus spoke to His disciples when He commissioned them and is speaking to us today.

"Go, therefore, and make disciples of all nations, baptizing them in the name of the Father, and of the Son, and of the holy Spirit, teaching them to observe all that I have commanded you. And behold, I am with you always, until the end of the age." Matthew 28:19-20

This is the mission that Jesus gave His disciples 2000 years ago and the mission He gives each of us today. Phrasing this passage into three distinct points, Jesus is telling us:

- Make Christians out of all My people by baptizing them.
- Teach them the moral code I taught you.
- Inspire them to live by this moral code.

The Pope Speaks

For starters, this is what Pope John Paul II had to say in his 1990 Encyclical Letter, "Mission of The Redeemer."

"The mission of Christ the Redeemer, which is entrusted to the Church, is still very far from completion. As the second millennium after Christ's coming draws to an end an overall view of the human race shows that this mission is still only beginning and that we must commit ourselves wholeheartedly to its service. It is the Spirit who impels us to proclaim the great works of God."[36]

This is a discouraging statement considering we have been at it for 2000 years. Have things improved any since 1990?

Disturbing Facts

Consider these facts and statistics for the United States and judge for yourself. I believe it is safe to assume conditions are about the same or even worse in other areas of the world.

- According to the Paulist Fathers and the Gallop Poll there are in the United States::
    63 million Catholics
    25 million are marginal-attend less than 6 masses a year
    18 million Catholics are estranged from the Church
    50 million Protestants are inactive or marginal
    65 million with no church affiliation - are unchurched
  This means that 58 % of the U.S. population is either inactive, marginal or unchurched.

- Looking at it from another point of view: during the past 10 years Catholic population has increased 21%. This sounds great until you consider that as a percent of total population it is virtually the same, increased by only 4 tenths of a percent.

- Even the 9/11/01 tragedy did little to effect the religious attitudes of United States citizens, except perhaps, for those who were directly effected. Even though we heard much about increased attention to prayer and special services, the internal effect was short lived. In some ways we were back to business as usual. Consider these figures compiled by Gallop:

	Prior To 9/11/01	November 2001	December 2001
Attended Church or Synagogue Regularly	41%	47%	42%
Religion Important To Them, Solves Problems	60%	64%	60%

The accuracy of these changes could be challenged but the size probably cannot, they support the previous figure of 58% of the United States population that needs to be evangelized.

Considering that Jesus instructed us to teach his moral code and how it should be obeyed, what do these Detroit News headlines tell us about our success in helping Jesus with His mission:

• "Dearborn women shoots 4 year old twins, then herself"

• "Teen who flew plane into Florida Building backed Terrorists"

• "Rink Rage: Hockey dad beats son's coach to death"

• "Teacher charged in sex assault on student"

• "Teen pleads guilty to killing his best friend"

• "Use of the drug ecstasy, among teens, is up 71% in 2 years"

• "Church In Crisis: Priest Sex Abuse"

Without fail, almost daily, newspapers have headlines about **murder, abortion, child abuse, theft, greed, suicide bombers,**

perverted sex, drug use; it goes on and on. There does not seem
to be any chance of these events being stopped or slowed down
significantly. Dr. James Dobson, a leading Protestant radio
personality, tells us, moral decay is flooding the U. S. like a burst
dam and the force of water cannot be stopped and picks up power
as it moves.

Many Good People

All this, even though true, is very negative and could leave the
impression nothing is being done to improve the situation. That's
not true, as there are millions of people working very hard doing
what they think needs to be done to correct the situation. Over the
years there have been millions of rosaries said, adoration hours put
in, novenas said, masses attended and prayers said but we still have
a very immoral situation in our country. I am not saying that these
efforts have not had a good effect. They certainly have. I hate to
think what the situation would be if this effort had not taken place.
So, what is the cause of all the evil in the world considering all the
effort that is being made to eliminate it?

Satan, The Evil One

To better understand why we need the full strength of the Holy
Spirit in our lives and the life of the Church, we must understand
the strength of Satan in our lives and the life of the Church. Who is
Satan, also known as the Devil and The Evil One? The Catechism
of the Catholic Church defines Satan as follows:

"Satan or the devil and the other demons are fallen angels
who have freely refused to serve God and his plan. Their
choice against God is definitive. They try to associate man
in their revolt against God." CCC 414

"In this petition,[1] evil is not an abstraction, but refers to a
person, Satan, the Evil One, the angel who opposes God.
The devil (*dia-bolos*) is the one who 'throws himself

across' God's plan and his work of salvation accomplished in Christ." CCC 2851

We look to the Catechism and the Bible for some very specific characteristics of Satan:

"'A murderer from the beginning,... a liar and the father of lies,' Satan is 'the deceiver of the whole world.'"[2] CCC 2852

"...By our first parents' sin, the devil has acquired a certain domination over man, even though man remains free. Original sin entails 'captivity under the power of him who thenceforth had the power of death, that is, the devil.'[3] ..." CCC 407

"You belong to your father the devil and you willingly carry out your father's desires. He was a murderer from the beginning and does not stand in truth, because there is no truth in him. When he tells a lie, he speaks in character, because he is a liar and the father of lies." John 8:44

"Be sober and vigilant. Your opponent the devil is prowling around like a roaring lion looking for [someone] to devour." First Peter 5:8

"And no wonder, for even Satan masquerades as an angel of light." Second Corinthians 11:14

Responses To Satan

These are very impressive credentials for a tempter, enticer, one who wants others to do evil. Throughout history there have been those who accept and those who reject the invitation of Satan to act on his evil offers, usually disguised as good. Our first parents, Adam and Eve, accepted his invitation to eat the forbidden fruit thus, committing a grave sin.

"Behind the disobedient choice of our first parents lurks a seductive voice, opposed to God, which makes them fall into death out of envy.[4] Scripture and the Church's Tradition see in this being a fallen angel, called 'Satan,' or the 'devil'[5]..." CCC 391

"...The serpent asked the woman, 'Did God really tell you not to eat from any of the trees in the garden?' The woman answered the serpent: 'We may eat of the fruit of the trees in the garden; it is only about the fruit of the tree in the middle of the garden that God said, "You shall not eat it or even touch it, lest you die."' But the serpent said to the woman: 'You certainly will not die! No, God knows well that the moment you eat of it your eyes will be opened and you will be like gods who know what is good and what is bad.' The woman saw that the tree was good for food, pleasing to the eyes, and desirable for gaining wisdom. So she took some of its fruit and ate it; and she also gave some to her husband, who was with her, and he ate it."
Genesis 3:1-6

Jesus Christ is the supreme example of one rejecting Satan's evil disguised as good when he rejected three such offers made to Him by Satan in the desert. Jesus is our model for dealing with Satan's evil offers.

"The Gospels speak of a time of solitude for Jesus in the desert immediately after his baptism by John. Driven by the Spirit into the desert, Jesus remains there for forty days without eating; he lives among wild beasts, and angels minister to him.[6] At the end of this time Satan tempts him three times, seeking to compromise his filial attitude toward God. Jesus rebuffs these attacks, which recapitulate the temptations of Adam in Paradise and of Israel in the desert, and the devil leaves him 'until an opportune time.'"[7] CCC538

"Filled with the holy Spirit, Jesus returned from the Jordan [after His baptism] and was led by the Spirit into the desert for forty days, to be tempted by the devil. He ate nothing during these days, and when they were over he was hungry." Luke 4:1-2

Devil: "If you are the Son of God, command this stone to become bread." Jesus: "It is written, 'One does not live by bread alone.'" Luke 4:3-4

Devil: "I shall give to you all this power [kingdoms of the world] and their glory; for it has been handed over to me, and I may give it to whomever I wish. All this will be yours, if you worship me." Jesus: "It is written:
'You shall worship the Lord, your God,
   and him alone shall you serve.'" Luke 4:5-8

Devil: "If you are the Son of God, throw yourself down from here [temple parapet], for it is written:
'He will command his angels concerning you,
   to guard you,' and:
'With their hands they will support you,'
   lest you dash your foot against a stone.'"
Jesus: "It also says, 'You shall not put the Lord, your God, to the test.'" Luke 4:9-12

"When the devil had finished every temptation, he departed from him for a time.
Jesus returned to Galilee in the power of the Spirit, and news of him spread throughout the whole region."
Luke 4:13-14.

The Solution

As I conclude this chapter there are two events that summarize the
evil situation in our country and motivates me to go forward with
all my energy to complete this book:

At the memorial service for kidnaped and murdered
Samantha Runnion, held July 24, 2002, Sheriff Leroy D.
Baca of LA County referred to Samantha as all that is good
in the world and what happened to her as all that is evil in
the world. Dr. Robert A. Schuller, of the Crystal Cathedral,
in his sermon pointed out that we all have a free will to
choose love (good) or evil; what makes us choose evil?

Former Mayor Rudy Giuliani was a guest on the 7/26/02
Good Morning America Program. Charlie Gibson asked
him about our solution to the events of 9/11/01 and all the
other evil events going on in the world. The Mayor
responded that what we are doing is an imperfect solution
to the problem. There really was no alternative solution
offered, there was almost a sense of despair as to what an
effective solution would be.

The Devil is on a raging campaign to spread his evil in the
world and overcome good. Despite all the efforts that are being
made spiritually, new laws, new programs, new security and many
other human efforts, the Devil's rage seems to be on the increase
and it seems no one knows how to stop it.

Jesus knew from the beginning that our human efforts would
not be powerful enough to battle the Devil and his deceiving ways.
He knew that we would need the same power of the Holy Spirit
that He had to help Him carry out His mission on this earth. Here
are Jesus' actual words spoken to us in scripture:

"After this the Lord appointed seventy[-two] others whom
he sent ahead of him in pairs to every town and place he

intended to visit....'Go on your way; behold, I am sending you like lambs among wolves.'" Luke 10:1, 3

"The seventy[-two] returned rejoicing, and said, 'Lord, even the demons are subject to us because of your name.' Jesus said, 'I have observed Satan fall like lightning from the sky. Behold, I have given you the power "to tread upon serpents" and scorpions and upon the full force of the enemy and nothing will harm you.'" Luke 10:17-19

The very last instructions Jesus gave His disciples before His ascension relates back to what He told the seventy-two in Luke 10:19-20. He wanted to be sure they understood the power they, as we do today, needed to carry out the mission he assigned to His people. Luke states it in these words:

"And [behold] I am sending the promise of my Father [the Holy Spirit] upon you; but stay in the city until you are clothed with power from on high." Luke 24:49

"But you will receive power when the holy Spirit comes upon you, and you will be my witnesses in Jerusalem, throughout Judea and Samaria, and to the ends of the earth." Acts 1:8

The mission of this book is to help the Body of Christ, the Church, to better understand this power Jesus offers us, its source, nature, how we get this power and how we use this power effectively to restore the world to what God intends it to be.

Some Final Thoughts

There are four important points I want to make before launching into the heart of this book. Your knowledge of these points will put into context what I am saying and increase your understanding of what I am saying:

16

One: Before Vatican II the Holy Spirit was often referred to as "The Lost Person of the Blessed Trinity" and reference to His gifts or the Pauline Charisms were not spoken of. Vatican II changed this as a result of a serious debate between Cardinal Suenens of Brussels, Belgium and Cardinal Ruffini of Palermo, Italy. Suenens argued for inclusion of the charisms and Ruffini argued against, saying their need had ceased. Cardinal Suenens position prevailed by a large margin and mention of the charisms is included in four council documents. This is strong support for Suenen's contention that the Catholic Church is both a Sacramental and Charismatic Church. This is what is said in the Dogmatic Constitution On The Church and clarified in the Catechism Of The Catholic Church:

"It is not only through the sacraments and the ministrations of the Church that the Holy Spirit makes holy the people, leads them and enriches them with His virtue. Allotting His gifts according to His will, He also distributes special graces among the faithful of every rank. By these gifts He makes them fit and ready to undertake various tasks and offices for the renewal and building up of the Church...Whether these charisms be very remarkable or more simple and widely diffused, they are to be received with thanksgiving and consolation since they are fitting and useful for the needs of the Church..."[37] Emphasis Added

"Grace is first and foremost the gift of the Spirit who justifies and sanctifies us. But grace also includes the gifts that the Spirit grants us to associate us with His work, to enable us to collaborate in the salvation of others and in the growth of the Body of Christ, the Church. There are *sacramental graces*, gifts proper to the different sacraments. There are furthermore *special graces*, also called *charisms* after the Greek term used by St. Paul and meaning 'favor,' 'gratuitous gift,' 'benefit.'[8] Whatever their character - sometimes it is extraordinary, such as the gift of miracles or of tongues-charisms are oriented toward sanctifying grace and are intended for the common good of the Church. They are at the service of charity which builds up the Church."⁹ CCC 2003

Two: The role of the natural vs. supernatural in God's plan of salvation has often been misused or misunderstood. Different groups have gone to opposite extremes; either one's natural talents and skills are all that counts or it is only supernatural grace like the charisms that count and they destroy the natural. Catholic Church doctrine is that both are important elements in our salvation, and that graces perfect the natural. How these two elements work in concert has been best described by Father Francis A. Sullivan, S.J. in his book, Charisms and Charismatic Renewal, A Theological and Biblical Study. Father Sullivan is the theologian who participated in preparing a position statement used by Cardinals Suenens in his debate with Cardinal Ruffini in their Vatican II debate on the charisms. The position this book takes on the matter of natural vs. supernatural is that expressed by Father Sullivan in this statement made in the introduction of his book:

"The charism as such is a gift of grace; it is the grace factor that enters into charismatic activity. But it will not be the only component of this activity. In every case the gift of grace will presuppose, build upon, and perfect the natural capacities that are already present. The special grace, which is the charism, as such, will add some new capacity and new readiness to undertake the activity for which it is given."³⁸

Three: It is important for one to recognize that gifts of the Holy Spirit, the charisms, working through us does not make us some sort of super human. We must allow Jesus to <u>work through us</u> with His power as expressed by the charisms. St. Paul recognized this by making this statement which applies to all of us:

"Three times I begged the Lord about this [thorn in my side], that it might leave me, but he said to me, 'My grace is sufficient for you, for power is made perfect in

weakness.' I will rather boast most gladly of my
weaknesses in order that the power of Christ may dwell
with me. Therefore, I am content with weaknesses, insults,
hardships, persecutions, and constraints, for the sake of
Christ; for when I am weak, then I am strong."
Second Corinthians 12:8-10.

Four: I want it understood that the purpose of this book is not to
promote the Catholic Charismatic Renewal. The Renewal has done
much to reintroduce the Charismatic Dimension of the Church but
there is still a long way to go before this restoration is complete.
The purpose of this book is to speak to the wider Church so they
will understand, accept and act on the Charismatic Dimension of
the Church.

Remember, it is only the power of God given to us by the Holy
Spirit and working through each of us that evil in the world can be
defeated. The balance of this book talks about this power, how
each of us can receive it and how to use it.

Chapter 3

The Holy Spirit Third But Not Last

Introduction

Before we can thoroughly understand the power the Father and Jesus offer us through the Holy Spirit, we must understand who the Spirit is, what He is, what He can do and how He operates. The purpose of this chapter is to answers these questions. The Catechism of the Catholic Church says this about the Holy Spirit:

> "*The Trinity is One.* We do not confess three Gods, but one God in three persons, the 'consubstantial Trinity.'[10] The divine persons do not share the one divinity among themselves but each of them is God whole and entire: 'The Father is that which the Son is, the Son that which the Father is, the Father and the Son that which the Holy Spirit is, i.e., by nature one God'[11] ..." CCC 253

> "*The divine persons are really distinct from one another.* 'God is one but not solitary.'[12] 'Father,' 'Son,' 'Holy Spirit' are not simply names designating modalities of the divine being, for they are really distinct from one another: 'He is not the Father who is the Son, nor is the Son he who is the Father, nor is the Holy Spirit he who is the Father or the Son.'[13] They are distinct from one another in their relations of origin: 'It is the Father who generates, the Son who is begotten, and the Holy Spirit who proceeds.'[14] The divine Unity is Triune." CCC 254

In summary, the Holy Spirit is totally God and equal to the Father and the Son in all ways. No human, regardless of how holy a person they are can even begin to be equal to the Holy Spirit. He

is often described as the great love that exists between the Father
and the Son and was assigned by Them to be our Advocate.

Many find it difficult to identify with the Holy Spirit because
we lack a human image of Him as we have for the Father and the
Son. It is difficult for us to identify with a dove, wind, fire so we
turn our attention to Him for whom there is a human image God
the Father and God the Son, Jesus Christ. Keep reminding yourself
that the Holy Spirit is a person the same as the Father and Son.
Based on the information given in this chapter on the Holy Spirit, I
suggest you form an image of Him in your mind that will remind
you how great and important a person He is to each of us.

The Old Testament

The Spirit or Holy Spirit is mentioned 55 times in the Old
Testament. Translated from the Hebrew word rûah the Holy Spirit
is often referred to as; wind, fire, water, breath. He played a key
role in creation and in the following verse wind refers to the Spirit
of God or the Holy Spirit:

"In the beginning, when God created the heavens and the
earth, the earth was a formless wasteland, and darkness
covered the abyss, while a mighty <u>wind</u> swept over the
waters.
Then God said, 'Let there be light,' and there was light."
Genesis 1:1-2, emphasis added

There is a major difference in how the Holy Spirit was used in
the Old Testament than in the New Testament. In the Old
Testament, the Spirit was given individually to specific people to
accomplish a specific task. In the New Testament, the Holy Spirit
is made available to "all God's People." Here are two examples
from the Old Testament of the Holy Spirit being given to specific
people for a specific task:

"Balaam, however, perceiving that the LORD was pleased to bless Israel, did not go aside as before to seek omens, but turned his gaze toward the desert. When he raised his eyes and saw Israel encamped, tribe by tribe, the spirit of God came upon him, and he gave voice to his oracle."
Numbers 24:1-3

"As she [Susanna] was being led to execution, God stirred up the holy spirit of a young boy named Daniel, and he cried aloud: 'I will have no part in the death of this woman.... Are you such fools, O Israelites! To condemn a woman of Israel without examination and without clear evidence?'"
Daniel 13:45-48

A prophecy that is very important to the Church today comes from Isaiah. It tells us about the coming of the Messiah; His origin and some of the important characteristics He will possess. This passage gives us the six traditional gifts of the Holy Spirit that we receive in the sacrament of confirmation

"But a shoot shall sprout from the stump of Jesse,
   and from his roots a bud shall blossom.
The spirit of the LORD shall rest upon him:
   a spirit of wisdom and of understanding,
A spirit of counsel and of strength,
   a spirit of knowledge and of fear of the LORD,"
Isaiah 11:1-2

Another very important prophesy for the New Testament Church and the Church today, comes from Joel. It announces that in the future God will not only give His Spirit selectively but to all mankind. This means that each one of us can have the power of the Holy Spirit available to work through us and help carry out our responsibility as a member of the "Body of Christ".

"Then afterward I will pour out
my spirit upon all mankind.
Your sons and daughters shall prophesy,
your old men shall dream dreams,
your young men shall see visions;
Even upon the servants and the handmaids,
in those days, I will pour out my spirit." Joel 3:1-2

The New Testament

The Holy Spirit is mentioned 231 times in the New Testament.
I have selected several of these passages to help explain the very
important role the Holy Spirit plays in our life and the Church. One
of these entries describes the Pentecost event, another Peter's
Pentecost speech when he quotes Joel's prophecy about the Holy
Spirit being made available to everyone:

"When the time for Pentecost was fulfilled, they were all in
one place together. And suddenly there came from the sky
a noise like a strong driving wind, and it filled the entire
house in which they were. Then there appeared to them
tongues as of fire, which parted and came to rest on each
one of them. And they were all filled with the holy Spirit
and began to speak in different tongues, as the Spirit
enabled them to proclaim."
Acts 2:1-4

"No, this is what was spoken through the prophet Joel:
'It will come to pass in the last days,' God says,
'that I will pour out a portion of my spirit upon all flesh.
Your sons and your daughters shall prophesy,
your young men shall see visions,
your old men shall dream dreams.
Indeed, upon my servants and my handmaids
I will pour out a portion of my spirit in those days,
and they shall prophesy." Acts 2:16-18

Pope John Paul II in his book, The Spirit Giver of Life and Love, said this about the birth of the Church. It was the power of the Holy Spirit promised to us by the Father and Son that empowered the Church to become visible and active in the world.

"The Church, which originated in Christ's redemptive death, was manifested to the world on Pentecost Day by the work of the Holy Spirit."[39]

"The Church was made manifest to the world on the day of Pentecost by the outpouring of the Holy Spirit.[15] The gift of the Spirit ushers in a new era in the 'dispensation of the mystery' - the age of the Church, during which Christ manifests, makes present, and communicates his work of salvation through the liturgy of his Church, 'until he comes.'[16] ..." CCC 1076

He gives the gift of Grace to us and the Church. Some of these graces are called charisms and will be the subject of later chapters. The Catechism of the Catholic Church tells us:

"Charisms are to be accepted with gratitude by the person who receives them and by all members of the Church as well. They are a wonderfully rich grace for the apostolic vitality and for the holiness of the entire Body of Christ, provided they really are genuine gifts of the Holy Spirit and are used in full conformity with authentic promptings of this same Spirit, that is, in keeping with charity, the true measure of all charisms."[17] CCC 800

"The grace of Christ is the gratuitous gift that God makes to us of his own life, infused by the Holy Spirit into our soul to heal it of sin and to sanctify it. It is the *sanctifying* or *deifying grace* received in Baptism. It is in us the source of the work of sanctification:[18] ..." CCC1999

It is the power of the Holy Spirit that gave us <u>Jesus, the Word Incarnate</u>, by the Virgin Motherhood of Mary and under the protection of Joseph, Jesus' Foster Father:

> "Now this is how the birth of Jesus Christ came about. When his mother Mary was betrothed to Joseph, but before they lived together, she was found with child through the holy Spirit. Joseph her husband, since he was a righteous man, yet unwilling to expose her to shame, decided to divorce her quietly. Such was his intention when, behold, the angel of the Lord appeared to him in a dream and said, 'Joseph, son of David, do not be afraid to take Mary your wife into your home. For it is through the holy Spirit that this child has been conceived in her.'. . .When Joseph awoke, he did as the angel of the Lord had commanded him and took his wife into his home." Matthew 1:18-20, 24

A central belief of the Catholic Church is that Jesus offered His Body and Blood to those who believe in Him to be their spiritual food and drink and lead them to salvation. This process is called <u>Transubstantiation</u>. The Holy Spirit represents the power that <u>changes</u> the bread and wine into the Body and Blood of Jesus when the priest invokes the Spirit to do so. There are not specific words to this effect in the bible, but this belief is a capital 'T' Tradition that has been held from the earliest days of the Church. That this is a fact is supported by Cyril of Jerusalem, The Catechism of the Catholic Church, and the Roman Missal:

> "Then having sanctified ourselves by these spiritual songs, we call upon the benevolent God to send out the Holy Spirit upon the gifts which have been laid out: that He may make the bread the Body of Christ, and the wine the Blood of Christ; for whatsoever the Holy Spirit touches, that is sanctified and changed."[40]

> "In the *epiclesis*,[19] the Church asks the Father to send his Holy Spirit (or the power of his blessing[20]) on the bread

and wine, so that by his power they may become the body
and blood of Jesus Christ and so that those who take part in
the Eucharist may be one body and one spirit. . . .
In the *institution narrative*, the power of the words and the
action of Christ, and the power of the Holy Spirit, make
sacramentally present under the species of bread and wine
Christ's body and blood, his sacrifice offered on the cross
once for all." CCC 1353

"And so Father, we bring you these gifts. We ask you to
make them holy by the power of Your Spirit, that they may
become the body and blood of your Son, our Lord Jesus
Christ, at whose command we celebrate this Eucharist."
Eucharistic Prayer No. 3.[41]

Jesus Christ was our first Advocate and knowing that when He
ascended back to His Father we would still need an Advocate here
on earth, He promised to send us the Holy Spirit that would be our
second Advocate. In some translations of the bible, the Paraclete
is used rather than Advocate. Jesus as our Advocate did many
things for us. So does and will the Holy Spirit do many things for
us as our Advocate: Intercessor, Defense Attorney, Spokesman,
Mediator, Comforter, Counselor, Teacher of Truth and Witness to
Jesus. He also represents Jesus on earth. What an impressive list.
Remember the Holy Spirit is a free gift from the Father and Son:

"And I will ask the Father, and he will give you another
Advocate to be with you always, the Spirit of truth, which
the world cannot accept, because it neither sees nor knows
it. But you know it, because it remains with you, and will
be in you.
The Advocate, the holy Spirit that the Father will send in
my name - he will teach you everything and remind you of
all that [I] told you." John 14:16-17, 26

"But I tell you the truth, it is better for you that I go. For if I
do not go, the Advocate will not come to you. But if I go, I

will send him to you. And when he comes he will convict the world in regard to sin and righteousness and condemnation: But when he comes, the Spirit of truth, he will guide you to all truth. He will not speak on his own, but he will speak what he hears, and will declare to you the things that are coming. He will glorify me, because he will take from what is mine and declare it to you." John 16:7-8, 13-14

A very important role of the Holy Spirit in the life of each of us is to be our <u>Sanctifier</u>. Sanctification is the process of personal supernatural transformation that starts at our Baptism when we become "A New Person" and continues until our life on this earth comes to an end. We become holy as God is holy so that we can be fit company for Him for all time. It is the Holy Spirit that both instructs and empowers one to live a Christ-like life. Both scripture and the Catechism confirm this for us:

"But we ought to give thanks to God for you always, brothers loved by the Lord, because God chose you as the firstfruits for salvation through sanctification by the Spirit and belief in truth. To this end he has [also] called you through our gospel to possess the glory of our Lord Jesus Christ." Second Thessalonians 2:13-14

"Sanctifying grace makes us 'pleasing to God.' Charisms, special graces of the Holy Spirit, are oriented to sanctifying grace and are intended for the common good of the Church. God also acts through many actual graces, to be distinguished from habitual grace which is permanent in us." CCC 2024

One of the greatest and most valuable gifts the Holy Spirit offers us are the <u>Fruits of the Spirit</u>. These are perfections that form within us as a result of our being docile to Him, listening to His instructions for us, and acting on these instructions. They are the "First fruits of our eternal glory." Paul tells us in Galatians we are in a continuing battle to suppress our desire for the fruits of the flesh. God made us to seek the fruits of the Spirit:

"....The fruit of the Spirit is love, joy, peace, patience, kindness, generosity, faithfulness, gentleness, self-control. Against such there is no law." Galatians 5:22-23

"By their fruits you will know them. Do people pick grapes from thornbushes, or figs from thistles? Just so, every good tree bears good fruit, and a rotten tree bears bad fruit. A good tree cannot bear bad fruit, nor can a rotten tree bear good fruit. Every tree that does not bear good fruit will be cut down and thrown into the fire. So by their fruits you will know them." Matthew 7:16-20

"By this power of the Spirit, God's children can bear much fruit. He who has grafted us onto the true vine will make us bear the 'fruit of the Spirit:...'[21] 'We live by the Spirit'; the more we renounce ourselves, the more we 'walk by the Spirit.'"[22] CCC 736

You would think that after all the Holy Spirit has offered to do for us and will do for us, that would be enough. But not so, He also wants to make His home in us, in our very bodies. What greater honor could God pay us, that the Third Person of the Blessed Trinity resides within us. My Pastor, Msgr. Tocco, said in one of his homilies, "if you want your body to be the home for the Holy Spirit you must keep it spiritually clean":

"Do you not know that your body is a temple of the holy Spirit within you, whom you have from God, and that you are not your own?" First Corinthians 6:19

What a resume! We should hire Him full-time to help us achieve the mission Jesus gave us, Matthew 28:19-20:

- Make Christians of all My people by baptizing them.
- Teach them the moral code I taught you.
- Inspire them to live by this moral code.

It is only His supernatural power that can give us the power we need to achieve this mission.

There is one final but very important point that must be made as this chapter comes to an end. It serves to tell just how important the Holy Spirit is in God's plan for our salvation. Jesus tells us what this is in the following words:

"Therefore, I say to you, every sin and blasphemy will be forgiven people, but blasphemy against the Spirit will not be forgiven. And whoever speaks a word against the Son of Man will be forgiven; but whoever speaks against the holy Spirit will not be forgiven, either in this age or in the age to come." Matthew 12: 31-32

The International Bible Commentary, which has the Nihil obstat and Imprimatur of the Catholic Church, makes this statement about Matthew 12:31-32:

"Blasphemy against the Holy Spirit-that is, deliberately resisting the working of God's Spirit and refusing to acknowledge the Spirit's power-is unforgivable. One may fail to recognize that Jesus is God's Servant, but deliberately to reject the working of the Spirit is to put oneself outside the kingdom."[42]

The power of the Holy Spirit empowered Jesus to have a successful three year mission on earth. It will do the same for His Church, the People of God. Let us really try it!!

Chapter 4

Power, What is it?

Introduction

Power is a very popular word, especially in the 21st century because it suggests an image of control over ourselves and others. The dictionary definition of power:

"Power is every quality, property or faculty by which any physical, natural or mechanical change, effect or result is produced. The ability or capacity to act or perform effectively or exercise control." Synonyms are: authority, domination, control, potency, might, cleverness, force and strength.

There are several types of power: human power, including mental and physical; mechanical like a car engine; electrical like a generator. Most often power is thought of as human power. Unless you refer to a religion book you are not apt to read anything about God's power or supernatural power.

It is important to understand the varied terminology that can be used to identify supernatural power. God's power is what we are talking about which is also expressed as Holy Spirit power and is activated through the gifts of the Spirit or charisms. The charisms are often referred to as the "power tools" of the Holy Spirit.

Human Power

Most references to human power suggest that we have the power within us to do anything we want. Here are some examples that show America's obsession with power is very strong:

- Words used in a certain way are an exercise of power. Public speaking courses and sales courses advertise: "develop the art of persuasion", "learn to use your mind power", "influence others to your way of thinking." There's nothing wrong with this if used to help others and not just to promote your own self interest or benefit.

- A recent half hour paid advertisement on TV was promoting a "Personal Power II Course" with the promise that "You can have it all." The implication is that you alone under your own power can do anything you want to do and achieve anything with no outside help of any kind.

- A recent TV ad selling the Cadillac Seville flashed these words across the screen, "The Power Is Yours" as the words were spoken in a very deep and commanding voice.

- A recent Clint Eastwood movie was titled so that it appealed to our obsession with power, "Absolute Power".

- Here are the titles of only three of the dozens of books you will find in a library or bookstore on personal power: "Power Within You", "Your Own Power-Unleash the Force Within" and "Thought The Greatest Power Of All".

In itself, there is nothing wrong with any of the above except they fail to recognize that the source of our power is our God. This thinking of self power spills over into one's spiritual life. There is a tendency to think we can solve problems of the Devil with our own personal power. Listen to this conversation between Pilate and Jesus:

"So Pilate said to him, 'Do you not speak to me? Do you not know that I have power to release you and I have power to crucify you?' Jesus answered [him], 'You would have no power over me if it had not been given to you from above. . . .' " John 19:10-11

The Father and Son have promised us that God's power would be shared with us through the Holy Spirit so we can effectively help Jesus in His mission. They entrusted us to use this power properly.

Power in the Old Testament

In the Old Testament the word power is mentioned 344 times and Spirit or Holy Spirit 55 times. Some of these references did not refer to God's power but natural power. God used the Holy Spirit's power in a different way in the Old Testament than He did in the New Testament. In the Old Testament Holy Spirit power was given to specific people to carry out a specific task. In the New Testament Holy Spirit power was poured out on all mankind starting at the first Pentecost and continuing to each person as they are Baptized and Confirmed even to this day. Here are two examples from the Old Testament where Moses is given God's power to carry out a specific task of leadership:

"The LORD said to him, 'On your return to Egypt, see that you perform before Pharaoh all the wonders I have put in your power. I will make him obstinate, however, so that he will not let the people go. So you shall say to Pharaoh: Thus says the LORD: Israel is my son, my first-born. Hence I tell you: Let my son go, that he may serve me. If you refuse to let him go, I warn you, I will kill your son, your first-born.'" Exodus 4:21-23

Elisha was favored by receiving God's power to save the armies of Israel, Judah and Edom. Elisha's armies after seven days were in the desert with no water and soon would be defeated by the Moab army. The Lord was asked for a prophet and Elisha surfaced:

"'Now get me a minstrel [musician].'
When the minstrel played, the power of the LORD came
upon Elisha and he announced: 'Thus says the LORD,
"Provide many catch basins in this wadi" [dry stream bed].
For the LORD says, "Though you will see neither wind nor
rain, yet this wadi will be filled with water for you, your
livestock, and your pack animals to drink." '"
2 Kings 3:15-17:

Power in the Gospels

The word power is used 42 times and Holy Spirit 46 times in
the 4 Gospels. You may think God's power was much less used in
the days of Jesus but keep this fact in mind: the Old Testament
covers about 2,300 years and the Gospels about 3 years. From this
perspective, the word power is used much more often in the
Gospels. It was not until Pentecost that the Holy Spirit came upon
all God's people, thus, all but 4 of the references to power in the
Gospels relate to Jesus' exercise of the Holy Spirit's power.
Jesus possessed the fullness of the Holy Spirit from the moment
He was conceived in Mary's womb. He manifested the power of
the Spirit in His ministry which started after His baptism in the
Jordan.

"It happened in those days that Jesus came from Nazareth
of Galilee and was baptized in the Jordan by John. On
coming up out of the water he saw the heavens being torn
open and the Spirit, like a dove, descending upon him. And
a voice came from the heavens, 'You are my beloved Son;
with you I am well pleased.'" Mark 1:9-11

After His baptism, the Spirit led Jesus into the desert where He
was tempted three times by Satan before He started His ministry.

"Jesus returned to Galilee in the power of the Spirit, and
news of him spread throughout the whole region."
Luke 4:14

The following scriptures tell us about the nature of the power Jesus exercised; He knew that He had power, He was aware of when this power was being exercised through Him, and others recognized that He had this power:

"Then Jesus approached [the eleven disciples] and said to them, 'All power in heaven and on earth has been given to me.'" Matthew 28:18

"And a woman afflicted with hemorrhages for twelve years, who [had spent her whole livelihood on doctors and] was unable to be cured by anyone, came up behind him and touched the tassel on his cloak. Immediately her bleeding stopped. Jesus then asked, 'Who touched me?' While all were denying it, Peter said, 'Master, the crowds are pushing and pressing in upon you.' But Jesus said, 'Someone has touched me; for I know that power has gone out from me.'" Luke 8:43-46

"They were all amazed and said to one another, 'What is there about his word? For with authority and power he commands the unclean spirits, and they come out.'" Luke 4:36

As a prelude to the coming of the Holy Spirit and His power on those in the Upper Room at Pentecost, Jesus on four occasions gave this power to others; to the 12 apostles, to the 72 disciples, when He established the Sacrament of Penance and when He gave Peter and his successors the power to bind and loose:

"He summoned the Twelve and gave them power and authority over all demons and to cure diseases, and he sent them to proclaim the kingdom of God and to heal [the sick]." Luke 9:1-2

"Jesus said, 'I have observed Satan fall like lightning from the sky. Behold, I have given you [seventy-two disciples] the power 'to tread upon serpents' and scorpions and upon the full force of the enemy and nothing will harm you.'" Luke 10:18-19

"[Jesus] said to them again, 'Peace be with you. As the Father has sent me, so I send you.' And when he had said this, he breathed on them and said to them, 'Receive the holy Spirit. Whose sins you forgive are forgiven them, and whose sins you retain are retained.'" John 20:21-23

"I will give you [Peter] the keys to the kingdom of heaven. Whatever you bind on earth shall be bound in heaven; and whatever you loose on earth shall be loosed in heaven." Matthew 16:19

In his book "Let The Fire Fall" Father Michael Scanlan, T.O.R. Chancellor of Franciscan University, Steubenville, Ohio writes this about the power of the Holy Spirit:

"The Holy Spirit empowers, He equips us with gifts and abilities that are not our own. Nowhere is this empowering work of the Spirit clearer than in the gospel accounts of the Spirit's empowering of Jesus."[43]

One reason Jesus came to earth as a human was to live first hand what life was going to be like for His people and what they would be faced with after He went back to the Father. He knew we would need the power of the Holy Spirit to survive and complete His mission. His message to us just before His ascension:

"[Behold] I am sending the promise* of my Father upon you; but stay in the city until you are clothed with power from on high." Luke 24:49

*The footnote explains that *promise* refers to the Holy Spirit.

Power In Other New Testament Books

These 23 books include: Acts of the Apostles (1), Pauline Letters (13), Hebrews (1), Catholic Letters (7) and Revelation (1). They are a history of the first 100 years of the Catholic Church. As you would expect, because of the promise Jesus made before His ascension, the Holy Spirit is mentioned 185 times and power is mentioned 109 times. There is only space here to give you a "Bird's Eye View" of these 100 years and how the Holy Spirit and His power were put to work to build the Church. In view of this, I suggest that each one of you read and study these books, especially Acts and the Letters of Paul.

It is significant that Luke ended his gospel by telling us of the "promise of the Father" and opened Acts of the Apostles with the same message but with more specific terminology:

"But you will receive power when the holy Spirit comes upon you, and you will be my witnesses in Jerusalem, throughout Judea and Samaria, and to the ends of the earth." Acts 1:8

Luke's repetition of Jesus' message about the coming of the Holy Spirit stressed the importance of this event. It would be called Pentecost the day on which Jesus founded His Church and those in the Upper Room would continue His mission of love and peace.

It was 10 days after Jesus ascended to His Father that He kept His promise about sending the Holy Spirit and power on His disciples in the Upper Room:

"When the time for Pentecost was fulfilled, they were all in one place together. And suddenly there came from the sky a noise like a strong driving wind, and it filled the entire house in which they were. Then there appeared to them tongues as of fire, which parted and came to rest on each one of them. And they were all filled with the holy Spirit and began to speak in different tongues, as the Spirit enabled them to proclaim." Acts 2:1-4

Those in the Upper Room on Pentecost received the Holy Spirit and were empowered to preach the "Good News" with boldness..

An excellent example of how the apostles continued the work of Jesus is an event involving Peter and John and their encounter with a crippled beggar:

"When he saw Peter and John about to go into the temple, he asked for alms. But Peter looked intently at him, as did John, and said, 'Look at us.'...Peter said, 'I have neither silver nor gold, but what I do have I give you: in the name of Jesus Christ the Nazorean, [rise and] walk.' Then Peter took him by the right hand and raised him up, and immediately his feet and ankles grew strong." Acts 3:3-7

Stephen, the first Christian martyr, is an excellent example of how the power of the Holy Spirit can transform one into a dynamic disciple of Jesus Christ to carry out His mission:

"Now Stephen, filled with grace and power, was working great wonders and signs among the people. Certain members of the so-called Synagogue of Freedom, Cyrenians, and Alexandrians, and people from Cilicia and Asia, came forward and debated with Stephen, but they could not withstand the wisdom and the spirit with which he spoke." Acts 6:8-10

His debaters were no match for Stephen so they stirred up the people who drove him out of the city. As they were stoning Stephen to death he called out, "Lord Jesus receive my spirit".

The Council of Jerusalem in about 50 AD was the first Council of the Catholic Church attended by the apostles and presbyters. They met to settle the dispute regarding the necessity for Gentiles

to fulfill the Mosaic laws before they could become a Christian.
Judas and Silas were sent to deliver the decision of the Council:

"It is the decision of the holy Spirit and of us not to place
on you any burden beyond these necessities,...." Acts 15:28

The important lesson for the Church and each of us is how this
decision was made. The Holy Spirit was consulted and played an
important role in their decision making process.

I will end this chapter with two important lessons about the
Holy Spirit that the Church needs to observe, especially today
with all the evil in our world and the need for the Holy Spirit's
power to overcome this evil. Both of these relate back to Jesus
telling us that sins against the Holy Spirit are not forgivable:

"Do not quench the Spirit. Do not despise prophetic
utterances. Test everything; retain what is good."
First Thessalonians 5:19-21

"Whoever has ears ought to hear what the Spirit says to the
churches." Revelation 2: 29

Cardinal Suenens tells us, "The apostles received as their last
instructions from Jesus an order not to launch out on their own
initiative, but to wait for the promise of the Father: for Him who
would clothe them with power..."[56] If the Church, society, and
families have situations that are not according to the gospel maybe
we are trying to solve them with our own power. It is time for us to
turn more fully to the power of the Holy Spirit to speak to us and
help us solve our problems.

Effective Power!

Engineers who understand how a car engine functions will tell you it is very important to keep it in good tune to get the most out of the engine's potential power. To operate at its full power potential a car engine must have:

- Spark plugs that are clean and correctly gapped.
- A clean air cleaner.
- Wiring is properly insulated and connections secure.
- Fresh gas of correct octane.
- A computer that is operating correctly.
- An ignition system that is operating correctly.

These same engineers will tell you that if a six cylinder car has one cylinder that is not working properly and the other five are, the power loss is not 1/6 or 16.7% but double that or 33.4%. Power is very sensitive and easily effected.

My experience in management training and organizational development taught me that this same principle applies to individuals and organizations. If a person or organization is not perfectly tuned, the loss of power from their efforts will multiply, not arithmetically but geometrically.

For individuals and the Church to operate at the full power God offers and expects of us, the Holy Spirit is needed. All cylinders of the Church must be operating with a "perfect tune-up". A full steam of power that comes from the Sacramental and Charismatic Dimensions of the Church is needed for us to effectively carry out God's plan.

This book is about how to tune up individuals and the Church to generate the full power of the Holy Spirit.

Chapter 5

The Charisms-Holy Spirit Power

Introduction

The source of God's power for His people and the Church is the Holy Spirit. The Holy Spirit channels this power to us through the seven Sacraments and the gifts of the Holy Spirit, or charisms. The Sacraments are a very important part of the Catholic Church and most Catholics have been well educated in what the Sacraments are and what they do for us. What is not as familiar to most Catholics is that the Church has a Charismatic Dimension that also channels this power to us through the gifts of the Holy Spirit. The purpose of this chapter is to explain what is meant by "Charismatic," why it is important to the Church and its people, and a brief history. We will start with a quote from the Vatican II Document Lumen Gentium, Dogmatic Constitution On the Church, and the Catechism of the Catholic Church which clearly establishes the Charismatic Dimension of the Catholic Church as an accepted doctrine:

"It is not only through the sacraments and the ministrations of the Church that the Holy Spirit makes holy the People, leads them, and enriches them with His virtues. Allotting His gifts according to His will, He also distributes special graces among the faithful of every rank. By these gifts He makes them fit and ready to undertake various tasks and offices for the renewal and building up of the Church, as it is written, 'the manifestation of the Spirit is given to everyone for profit'. Whether these charisms be very remarkable or more simple and widely diffused, they are to be received with thanksgiving and consolation since they are fitting and useful for the needs of the Church. ... Those who have charge over the Church should judge the genuineness and proper use of these gifts, through their office not indeed to extinguish the Spirit, but to test all things and hold fast to what is good."[44] Emphasis Added

"Grace is first and foremost the gift of the Spirit who justifies and sanctifies us. But grace also includes the gifts that the Spirit grants us to associate us with his work, to enable us to collaborate in the salvation of others and in the growth of the Body of Christ, the Church. There are *sacramental graces*, gifts proper to the different sacraments. There are furthermore *special graces*, also called *charisms* after the Greek term used by St. Paul and meaning 'favor.' 'gratuitous gift,' 'benefit.'[23] Whatever their character - sometimes it is extraordinary, such as the gift of miracles or of tongues-charisms are oriented toward sanctifying grace and are intended for the common good of the Church. They are at the service of charity which builds up the Church.[24]" CCC 2003

What Are Charisms?

Charism comes from the Greek word charisma which means a gift or grace from the Holy Spirit. They directly or indirectly benefit the Church, the Body of Christ. Charismata is the word Paul used in First Corinthians when he wrote about "spiritual gifts". Charisms when activated, are manifestations of the Holy Spirit's power. Here are some of the characteristics of charisms:

- Charisms cannot be earned or developed, they are an absolutely free gift from the Holy Spirit.

- They do not include our natural skills and talents which we are born with and can develop. There is an important relationship between one's natural and supernatural gifts and talents. See page 17 for Father Sullivan's statement..

- They are given selectively and only when needed for a good purpose related to the mission of Jesus and our part in that mission.

- Paul makes it very clear that the charisms are to be sought and manifested only in the context of LOVE.

- Their purpose is not for individual gain but for building the Church and her people.

Following is a list of Charisms that will be developed in more detail in later chapters. They are divided into three categories:

FOUNDATION CHARISMS:
- Prayer - Petition of the Holy Spirit
- Faith - Assurance of the Holy Spirit
- Hope - Optimism of the Holy Spirit
- Love - Heart of the Holy Spirit
- Contemplation - Reflection of the Holy Spirit

ENABLING OR POWER CHARISMS
- Discernment - Judgement of the Holy Spirit
- Knowledge - Diagnosis of the Holy Spirit
- Wisdom - Prescription of the Holy Spirit
- Prophecy - Message of the Holy Spirit
- Exhortation - Persuasion of the Holy Spirit
- Boldness - Courage of the Holy Spirit

SERVICE CHARISMS:
- Administration
- Apostle
- Evangelization
- Giving

- Healing
- Helper
- Leadership
- Mercy
- Ministry
- Miracles
- Pastoring
- Teaching

We turn our attention to a brief history of the Charismatic Dimension of the Church. Even though the power of the Holy Spirit was very prevalent in the Old Testament, it was manifested through individuals selected by God. This is not the subject of this book.

New Testament & Early Post-Biblical Years

The following comments come from the study, "Christian Initiation And Baptism In The Holy Spirit-Evidence From The First Eight Centuries"[45]. The authors of this study are: Father George T. Montague, S.M.., Professor of Theology at St. Mary's University, San Antonio, Texas and Father Kilian McDonnell, O.S.B., President of the Institute for Ecumenical and Cultural Research, Collegeville, Minnesota. There follows, four observations based on this book. They are supported with two quotations from the book for each observation. The first quotation is from the section on the New Testament and the second from Early Post-Biblical section:

1. Those who participated in the rite of Christian Initiation experienced the reception of and manifestation of one or more charisms:

"George Montague re-examines the New Testament text and finds that the gift of the Spirit, including the charisms, was integral to Christian Initiation. In the Synoptics, the baptism of Jesus is the paradigm [model] for this Spirit-imparting grace of initiation. In Luke-Acts, the prophetic dimension of the Spirit predominates, but, despite opinions to the contrary, it is not possible to separate the gifts of the Spirit from integral initiation. Paul too understands the Holy Spirit to be given in Baptism and charismatic expression to be normal, though certainly not the only effect of the sacrament." From the Precis, [Abstract]

"Whether using the death and resurrection or the baptism of Jesus model, Tertullian, Hilary, Cyril, Basil, Gregory Nazianzus, John of Apemea, Philoxenous, Theodoret, Severus, and Joseph Hazzaya, in varying ways situate the imparting of the Spirit and the reception of the charisms within the rite of initiation....In every community the prophetic charisms of tongues, wisdom, healing were found. Prophets were numerous." Page 342

2. There was some external expression of receiving the Holy Spirit evoked during the Rite of Initiation, such as joy, happiness, praise etc:

"...it is clear from the paradigmatic [model] nature of Acts 2:1-38, 10:44-48 and 19:5 that not only the gift of the Spirit belongs essentially to Christian Initiation, but that some external expression of its reception is normal... Luke sees the charismatic expression as a marvelous confirmation of God's action in the event of Christian Initiation." Page 40

"More dramatic is Hilary's appeal to experience, namely, his own baptism. In bold, sentient language he writes of experiencing intense joy when the neophytes feel the first stirring of the Holy Spirit within. This movement of the Spirit within is expressed in charisms of knowledge, prophecy, wisdom, exorcism." Page 343

44

3. The manifestations of having received the Holy Spirit and initial charisms has an effect that goes far beyond being initiated:

"The initial gift of the Spirit is not static but is meant to grow. This appeared most clearly in our study of *anakainosis* [renewal] in Titus 3:5, and it is confirmed by 2 Corinthians 3:18. We may reasonably assume that such growth, like growth in nature, may be at times gradual and at other times dramatic." Page 89

"For John of Apamea [Syrian writer] one must "perfectly possess in oneself the power of holy baptism" then one will be "adorned with all the divine gifts." Further he places this empowerment through the actualized baptism..., so the charisms manifest themselves only after one has perfectly possessed the power of baptism." Page 357

4. Here are two important observations the authors made at the end of their portion of this study:

By Father Montague: "In all cases, the charismatic empowerment is destined not for personal fanfare but for the *building up of the church* and evangelization. The charismatic dimension of the Spirit's life is therefore crucial to the survival and growth of the Church. The gifts are not toys but tools. They are not optional accessories but part of the church's essential equipment for its upbuilding, and everyone baptized has received a charismatic grace to be ministered to the community." Page 90

By Father McDonnell: "In rather extensive literature on charism and institution it has become a dictum that institution without charism is death, while charism without institution is chaos. If the church were to attempt to live solely off the charismatic, it would be delivered to sectarian enthusiasm and fragmentation. Charism and institutions, when kept in mutuality, reciprocally discipline and support one another." Page 371

If, after reading and contemplating these eight pieces of evidence from this study, you are not convinced that the Charismatic Dimension of the Church is part of and needed by the Catholic Church to play a prominent role in carrying out the mission Jesus gave us, I suggest that you obtain a copy of the study. It has 382 pages of indisputable evidence.

The Charisms Seem To Disappear

The Charismatic Dimension of the Catholic Church started to fade in the fourth century but was still quite prominent into the eighth century as the study we just reviewed establishes. Although the charisms seemed to have disappeared, they had not, as we will understand when we consider they were active especially among the saints and desert fathers. What are the reasons that they did virtually disappear?

- When infant baptism became the norm, attention was taken away from the experience of baptism and receiving charisms of empowerment.

- As confirmation was separated from baptism to a later date in life there was still some stress on being empowered by the Holy Spirit but the emphasis was on the Isaiah 11:2-3 characteristics of the Messiah and not the Pauline charisms originally used in Initiation.

- The Montanist heresy so misused the charisms that they collided with Episcopal authority and thus the charisms became suspect by association with the heresy and restrictions were put on them.

- As the church grew it became more organized and regulated with its major attention on the Sacramental Dimension of the Church. Much of the Churche's effort needed to be put into defending its dogmas and attention was directed toward the Reformation and Council of Trent.

- Early century Christian liturgies were open to spontaneous charismatic expression, at appropriate times during the liturgy, by the assembly. It was common to hear; *praying in tongues;* word gifts such as *prophecy, word of knowledge, and word of wisdom; to see raising of hands in praise and worship.* This often happened in the Rite of Christian Initiation. The Mass in the early Church was often similar to the Mass of today that includes charismatic expression by the assembly. By the mid-fourth-century as the Church grew, its liturgies developed becoming more formalized with less participation by the assembly, and the language was eventually changed to Latin for the entire Church. Charismatic expression virtually disappeared from liturgies. Vatican II has done much to restore assembly understanding (vernacular), their participation, and charismatic expression.

The Saints and Charisms

Most saints can be given credit for helping keep the Charismatic Dimension of the Church alive. I will name only a few to give you a good idea of the contribution they made. Most books on the saints say little or nothing about the charisms they manifested. There are two books I know of that do an excellent job of this. One is Gathering a People-Catholic Saints In Charismatic Perspective by Judith Tydings. It is out of print. I found my copy through a used book dealer. The second, Miracles of the Saints, A Book of Reflections by Bert Ghezzi. Here are several of the many saints that had charisms and manifested them in their ministry:

- Saint Dominic, OP (1170-1221) the founder of the Dominican Order, the Order of Preachers. Known for the charisms of: healing, preaching, evangelization and miracles.

- Saint Catherine of Siena (1347-1380) a Doctor of the Church, influential in getting the Papacy returned to Rome from Avigonon, France and influential in overcoming the Great Western Schism when anti-popes tried to take over the Papacy. Known for the charisms of: poverty, healing, wisdom, knowledge, exhortation, prayer and tongues.

- Saint Teresa of Avila (1515-1582) the first woman Doctor of the Church and reformer of the Carmelite Order. Known for the charisms of prophecy, wisdom, knowledge, administration and tongues.

- Venerable Solanus Casey (1870-1957) although not yet declared a saint was known as "The Door Keeper" at the Capuchin St. Bonaventure Monastery in Detroit. Known for the charisms of humility, love, hope, miracles, knowledge, wisdom, and healing.

The Long Road Back

The Holy Spirit was often characterized as "The Lost Person of the Blessed Trinity." Although He was still active in the Church His power was being used in a limited way and there was very little written, spoken or taught about Him. For most Catholics He was known as the "Holy Ghost", something one received in Baptism and Confirmation but had very little understanding of what He was all about. Nevertheless, the Holy Spirit was covertly at work in the hearts and minds of select individuals who would be motivated to study, write about, and preach on the Holy Spirit. The following is a sampling of these people and what they wrote about the Church and the Spirit:

- Father Denis Petau, S.J. (1583-1652) a supporter of positive theology, considered one of the great theologians of all time. His writings on the Holy Spirit, although rejected by some, have with modification become accepted. In his book, The Trinity, he referred to the Holy Spirit as the <u>power</u> of the Father and the Son and that the substance of the Holy Spirit is joined with us in some mysterious and unusual way.

- Father Johann Adam Moehler (1796-1838) was a Catholic historian. He wrote about what he considered abuses of the Church including withholding the cup from the laity and using Latin in Catholic worship. He wrote about the Holy Spirit and that one's divine involvement in the life of the Church comes to us through the Holy Spirit.

- Father Matthias Joseph Scheeben (1835-1888) was educated at the Gregorian University in Rome. His great contribution was in speculative theology and is considered to be an extension of the writings of Father Petau on the role of the Holy Spirit in one's life. He taught that the Holy Spirit takes possession of us in a special way and he was far ahead of most theologians on the theology of the laity. He wrote in such a way that one did not need to be a theologian to understand what he was saying.

- Pope Leo XIII in 1893 played a key role in stirring the winds of renewal in the Church with his Encyclical, Providentissimu Deus, Study of Holy Scripture. This did much to reaffirm Scripture as the Word of God inspired by the Holy Spirit. It set down principles for interpreting the Bible.

- Pope Leo XIII again in 1897 wrote his Encyclical, Divium Illud Munus, The Holy Spirit. It decreed a novena to the Holy Spirit every year in every church in the world between Easter and Pentecost, a decree that has been virtually ignored, at least in my adult life time. It is significant that this was written as the result of a "word of knowledge" given to a lay person, a cook, in a convent of the Oblate Sisters of the Holy Spirit. The cook passed this word on to Mother Elena Guerra who literally stormed the Pope with communications until he wrote the Encyclical. She was the first person to be beatified by Pope John XXIII.

• Father Maurice De La Taille, S.J. (1872-1933) was a theologian in France and a Chaplain in World War I. He wrote a book, "Mysteries of the Faith", which related how the Last Supper and Cross complement each other. His principle thesis is not accepted today nor did it agree with the Council of Trent regarding the Mass. Even though his thesis was rejected, his book is considered a major contribution to Eucharistic theology. His writings on "created actuation by uncreated act" gave us a theory regarding the supernatural union of God with man are widely accepted today. His writings in this area complement and expand on the work of Father Scheeben regarding the action of the Holy Spirit in one's life.

• Cardinal Yves Congar, O.P.(1904-1995) a French Dominican who made a major contribution to the theology of the Holy Spirit both before, during and after Vatican II. In recognition of his contribution, Pope John Paul II made him a Cardinal in 1994. In 1951, he wrote "Lay People In The Church" in which he stressed that the charisms should be common place and are essential to the growth of the Church and the mission of Jesus.

• Cardinal Léon-Joseph Suenens (1904-1996). When he became Auxiliary Bishop of Malines-Bussels in 1945 he selected as his motto, "By The Holy Spirit From the Virgin Mary" and dedicated his life to this motto. Cardinal Suenens was a prime mover at Vatican II regarding getting the Charismatic Dimension of the Church strongly recognized in the Vatican II documents. His book, "The New Pentecost" is a classic in explaining this Charismatic Dimension.

50

- Pope Pius XII (1876-1958) in 1943 wrote his Encyclical Mystici Corporis Christi, The Mystical Body of Christ. This encyclical is important because it reminds us that Christ is the Church and that all of us are part of the Church. In this encyclical Pope Pius XII mentions the Holy Spirit 36 times and the charisms several times. This is what he said about the charisms, "No one, of course, can deny that the Holy Spirit of Jesus Christ is the one source of whatever supernatural power [charisms] enters into the Church and its members."

Blessed Pope John XXIII

Blessed Pope John XXIII (1881-1963) at age 77 was elected pope on October 28, 1958. Many thought of him as an interim selection but that is not what the Holy Spirit had in mind. Less than three months after his election he announced he was calling an Ecumenical Council and for a revision of the Code of Canon Law. There was nothing in his background that would lead anyone to believe he had this in mind. The Holy Spirit had plans for this holy man and gave him a word of wisdom regarding a Council. Pope John puts it this way in his book, Journey Of A Soul:

> "Without any forethought, I put forward in one of my first talks with my Secretary of State, on January 20, 1959, the idea of an Ecumenical Council, a Diocesan Synod and the revision of the Code of Canon Law, all this being quite contrary to any previous suppositions or ideas of my own on this subject."[46]

On January 25, 1959, the feast of St. Paul, he announced to 17 Cardinals at the Basilica of St. Paul his intention to convene Vatican II. On December 25, 1961 he made an official announcement in his Apostolic Letter Humanae Salutis of Vatican

II to start in 1962. He concluded this letter with the following prayer:

"Renew Your wonders in our times, as though for a new Pentecost, and grant that the Holy Church, preserving unanimous and continuous prayer, together with Mary, the mother of Jesus, and also under the guidance of St. Peter, may increase the reign of the Divine Savior, the reign of truth and justice, the reign of love and peace. Amen".[47]

He used the Italian word *Aggiornamento* to emphasize the purpose of the Council. In English, this word means "updating". It does not mean to change basic theology or dogmas of the Church but to make them better understood and accepted in the modern world. In the aftermath of the Council, the following practices of the early church were re-introduced or confirmed:

- Vernacular as a permissible language for Mass.

- The priest facing the people while saying Mass.

- Receive Eucharist in both species, Body and Blood.

- Receiving the Body of Christ in the throne of one's hands.

- Reviving the Charismatic Dimension of the Church.

After Vatican II

It is not my purpose in this book to cover Vatican II, except in relation to the Charismatic Dimension of the Church. One personal comment, I was 47 years old when they started to implement the Council. I have seen the best and worst of Pre and Post Vatican II. Once I experienced what the Post Vatican II Church has done for my faith and relationship with Jesus, I would, not trade this for my best experience of Pre Vatican II times.

The Charismatic Dimension of the Church is mentioned seven times in four Vatican II documents and the Holy Spirit is used more than 250 times. On page 39 of this chapter, I quote the reference found in the Dogmatic Constitution On The Church. There are two other similar references in this document. The Decree On The Apostolate Of The Lay People has two such references. The Decree On The Ministry And Life Of Priests and Decree On The Church's Missionary Activity have one reference each. Below I quote one passage from Lay People and one from Priests documents because they firmly stress the Charismatic Dimension of the Church:

"The Holy Spirit sanctifies the People of God through the ministry and sacraments. However, for the exercise of the apostolate He gives the faithful special gifts besides, allotting them to each one as He wills, so that each and all, putting at the service of others the grace received may be as good stewards of God's varied gifts, for the building up of the whole body in charity. From the reception of these charisms, even the most ordinary ones, there arises for each of the faithful the right and duty of exercising them in the Church and in the world for the good of men and the development of the Church, of exercising them in the freedom of the Holy Spirit who breathes where He wills. And at the same time in communion with his brothers in Christ, and with the pastors especially. It is for the pastors to pass judgement on the authenticity and good use of these gifts, not certainly with a view to quenching the Spirit but to test everything and keeping what is good."[48]
Emphasis Added

"While trying the spirit if they be of God, they [priests] must discover with faith, recognize with joy and foster with diligence the many and varied charismatic gifts of the laity, whether these be of a humble or more exalted kind. Among the other gifts of God which are found abundantly among the faithful, special attention ought to be devoted to those graces by which a considerable number of people are attracted to greater heights of the spiritual life."[49] Emphasis Added

So there is no misunderstanding, the seven references in the Vatican II documents to the charisms made it clear that they were referring primarily to the charisms, gifts of the Spirit that St. Paul wrote about in: Romans 12:7-8; 1 Corinthians 12:4-31, 13:1-13,14:1-40; Ephesians 4:11-12. The Isaiah 11:2-3 gifts are not specifically mentioned or referred to in the Council Documents.

A major event occurred in 1967 that dramatically opened the door for the Charismatic Dimension of the Church to flourish and take its needed place as a major factor along with the Sacramental Dimension to help the Church carry out its mission. It is referred to as the "Duquesne Weekend," a retreat held at Duquesne University February 17-19, 1967. It is recognized as the beginning of the Charismatic Renewal in the Catholic Church. A group of 29 including students, professors and a Catholic priest attended this retreat.

There was some anticipation of what would happen at this retreat because of some activities the participants took part in during the days prior to the retreat. They attended prayer meetings, read books on gifts of the Spirit, talked with Protestants involved in the charismatic renewal, and were involved with the Cursillo Movement. What happened was a "New Pentecost" for these people. As they were prayed over for a deeper filling of the Holy Spirit they began to experience God's great love for them, the power of the Holy Spirit in them, and an experience of one or more charisms. Their lives were changed forever.

There was a relationship between some of those at Duquesne and the University of Notre Dame, so very soon there were similar experiences at Notre Dame and from there the Catholic Charismatic Renewal literally spread all over the world. Similar activities of the Charismatic Renewal are going on in most every country of the world. For simplicity, this book is about the renewal in the United States. In most cases the renewal activity in other countries is modeled after the United States.

Involvement in the renewal exploded. Life in the Spirit Seminars were being conducted across the United States, in which people were prayed over for a greater filling of the Holy Spirit and manifestation of the charisms. This process was called Baptism in the Spirit. Since 1967, there are literally millions of Catholics in the U.S. who have been Baptized in the Spirit. Prayer Groups and Life in the Spirit Seminars flourished and the charisms began to reappear. Two Popes, Paul VI, John Paul II, and the U.S. Bishops have praised and endorsed the Charismatic Renewal but did very little toward getting it into the mainstream of the Church. There were all sorts of conferences, workshops, teachings being held on a Diocesan, State and National level. There is a small International Charismatic Renewal Office in Rome. It seemed that this was the answer to reestablishing the Charismatic Dimension of the Church as it was in the early centuries and making it a more powerful force in the world.

Consensus is that in 1980 the Catholic Charismatic Renewal peaked and started to decline. The number of Prayer Groups and Life in the Spirit Seminars started on a decline as did attendance at regional and national conferences. Even though the charisms were out of the closet they were manifested primarily in prayer meetings and other assemblies of those involved in the renewal. I became involved in 1988 and after a few years it became apparent to me that the Charismatic Renewal was not accomplishing what the Holy Spirit intended, to restore the Charismatic Dimension of the Church. It seemed unlikely that they had a vision that was in this direction or at least a plan to achieve such a vision.

It is not the purpose of this book to place blame on any person or organization or give reasons for this failure. The purpose of this book is to:

- Re-establish the validity of the Charismatic Dimension of the Catholic Church as an expression of the power of the Holy Spirit.

- To motivate the hierarchy, priests, influential lay people and the Renewal to start planning, organizing and implementing events that will accomplish this restoration.

The Vatican II Document on the "Lay People" makes it clear that there is an obligation for the people of God to accept and manifest the charisms.

"...there arises for each of the faithful the right and duty of exercising them (charisms) in the Church and in the world..."[48] Emphasis Added

It seems to follow that the Church has a right and duty to educate and guide its people in the nature and use of these charisms.

The next three chapters will deal with explaining in some detail the charisms, gifts of the Holy Spirit. The final two chapters will deal with how one receives these gifts and how they can be manifested by individuals and organizations.

We need to decide now to achieve the prayer expressed by Blessed Pope John XXIII as he opened the Second Vatican Council; "Renew Your wonders in this our day as by a new Pentecost." I am sure that Pope John would agree that this Pentecost, to be effective and lasting, must be a continuing event in one's life and not a once a year event.

56

Prayer for Power

"Do not pray for tasks

equal to your powers.

Pray for powers

equal to your tasks-

then the doing of your work

shall be no miracle

but you shall be a miracle."

From the prayer *"Life"* used by
Venerable* Father Solanus Casey, O.F.M. Cap.
In his ministry of counseling and healing.
He manifested these charisms:
Word of Knowledge and Wisdom,
Discernment and Prophecy,
Healing and Miracles.

*Father Solanus is a candidate for Beatification. His sponsor
would   like to hear from you regarding any miracles he is
responsible for since his death in 1957. Call Brother Richard at
1-313-579-2100

Chapter 6

Foundation Charisms

Introduction

If the Church, the People of God, are going to effectively continue the mission of Jesus, they must first have and portray an image of Jesus. This image of Jesus will include: Love, Faith, Hope, Prayer and Contemplation. For one to portray this image of Jesus, they need more that just the natural manifestation of these characteristics. They need the supernatural power of the Holy Spirit, or charisms, to exhibit the true nature of Jesus.

Love

Love is the HEART of the Holy Spirit. It is the love that exists between God the Father and God the Son, represented by God the Holy Spirit. It is the love the Father has for each one of us as expressed by His Son who died on the cross for our salvation:

"No one has greater love than this, to lay down one's life for one's friends." John 15:13

In turn, we are to accept God's love which is often very difficult, considering the things that happen to us and things we do that are not pleasing to God. An even more difficult task for us is to let the love we have received from God shine forth to others, even people we do not like:

"He said to them, 'You shall love the Lord, your God, with all your heart, with all your soul, and with all your mind. The second is like it. You shall love your neighbor as yourself.'" Matthew 22:37, 39

58

"But I say to you, love your enemies, and pray for those who persecute you." Matthew 5:44

The best and most complete description of charismatic love was given to us by St. Paul in his First Letter to the Corinthians.

"Love is patient, love is kind. It is not jealous, [love] is not pompous, it is not inflated, it is not rude, it does not seek its own interests, it is not quick-tempered, it does not brood over injury, it does not rejoice over wrongdoing but rejoices with the truth. It bears all things, believes all things, hopes all things, endures all things."
First Corinthians 13:4-7

This is a tough assignment St Paul gives us. That is why we need the power of the Holy Spirit to achieve charismatic love.

Faith

Faith is the ASSURANCE of the Holy Spirit. We are not talking about faith that comes from our natural experiences. If the traffic light is red, we have faith it will soon turn green and if by chance it does not, someone will fix it. We are not talking about the Catholic faith which are our beliefs based on scripture, Tradition, and the teaching of the Church. We are talking about our trust in and reliance on these teaching of the Catholic Church even if we do not fully understand them:

"...*Faith is a gift of God, a supernatural virtue infused by him.* 'Before this faith can be exercised, man must have the grace of God to move and assist him; he must have the interior helps of the Holy Spirit, who moves the heart and converts it to God, who opens the eyes of the mind and "makes it easy for all to accept and believe the truth.""'"
[25] CCC 153

Sometimes a negative example can prove a point. We all know the story of how the disciples were fishing and a storm came up and the boat was being tossed about. The disciples became even more terrified when a person came walking toward them on the water and they thought it was a ghost. Then this transpired:

"At once [Jesus] spoke to them, 'Take courage, it is I; do not be afraid.' Peter said to him in reply, 'Lord, if it is you, command me to come to you on the water.' He said, 'Come.' Peter got out of the boat and began to walk on the water toward Jesus. But when he saw how [strong] the wind was he became frightened; and, beginning to sink, he cried out, 'Lord, save me!' Immediately Jesus stretched out his hand and caught him, and said to him, 'O you of little faith, why did you doubt?'" Matthew 14: 27-31

Lesson: Jesus commanded Peter to walk on the water. Do you think that Jesus would do this and not see to it that Peter had the power to walk on water? Peter did not trust Him and took his eyes off Jesus. The following is an example that points out what Jesus says we can do if we trust Him. Jesus was hungry when He came upon a fig tree that had no fruit. He said to the tree, "Because of this you will never bear fruit" and it withered:

"Jesus said to them in reply, 'Amen, I say to you, if you have faith and do not waver, not only will you do what has been done to the fig tree, but even if you say to this mountain, "Be lifted up and thrown into the sea," it will be done.'" Matthew 21:21

"Faith in God leads us to turn to him alone as our first origin and our ultimate goal, and neither to prefer anything to him nor to substitute anything for him." CCC 229

Our intellect and will are involved in building faith [trust] in God and Catholic teaching. The intellect is the easier step in

60

gaining faith. It is in conforming our will to God's will that we have difficulties and need the special help of the Holy Spirit.

Hope

Hope is the OPTIMISM of the Holy Spirit. It is closely related to and follows faith. St. Paul made this very clear to us in one of his talks to the gentiles in Rome. He ended with these words:

"May the God of hope fill you with all joy and peace in your faith, so that in the power of the Holy Spirit, you may be rich in hope." Romans 15:13 (NJB)

Hope can be based on one's natural ability and efforts or on the supernatural power of the Holy Spirit. This supernatural power is based on the death and resurrection of Jesus Christ and His promise of salvation for each of us. Natural hope does not give one an absolute assurance that what is hoped for will happen. It leads one to continual thought, worry, prayer of petition, and wondering about the outcome. Supernatural hope also leads one to prayer but with a different purpose, thanksgiving and praise. It also leads one to some form of action that will pass on to others this grace of hope. The Catechism tells us:

"Hope is the theological virtue by which we desire the kingdom of heaven and eternal life as our happiness, placing our trust in Christ's promises and relying not on our own strength, but on the help of the grace of the Holy Spirit. 'Let us hold fast the confession of our hope without wavering, for he who promised is faithful.'[26] 'The Holy Spirit…he poured out upon us richly through Jesus Christ our savior, so that we might be justified by his grace and become heirs in hope of eternal life.'"[27] CCC1817

St. Paul tells us that the charism of hope is the power that keeps us going when the going gets tough. We all know people who seem to be so burdened with problems. We wonder how they can get out of bed in the morning and be so cheerful about it. Paul gives us the answer in these words:

"For in hope we were saved. Now hope that sees for itself is not hope. For who hopes for what one sees? But if we hope for what we do not see, we wait with endurance." Romans 8:24-25

Our first Pope, St. Peter, tells us we have a responsibility to others as a result of the hope the Holy Spirit has given us:

"....Always be ready to give an explanation to anyone who asks you for a reason for your hope, but do it with gentleness and reverence, keeping your conscience clear, so that, when you are maligned, those who defame your good conduct in Christ may themselves be put to shame." First Peter 3: 15-16

In this passage, Pope Peter is also talking to us about endurance as St. Paul did in Romans.

A person I admire because of what he did for the Catholic Church, because of his trust in the Holy Spirit and the gift of hope he received from the Spirit is Léon Joseph Cardinal Suenens (1904-1996), former Archbishop of Malines-Brussels, Belgium. He was a close confidant of Popes John XXIII, Paul VI. and John Paul II. He was one of the moderators of Vatican Council II, and a leading force responsible for getting the Charismatic Dimension of the Church accepted by the Council and written about in several documents. He was a great supporter of lay people and had much to do with formulating the document, Decree on the Apostolate of Lay People. Not talked or written about was the suffering he endured in his 92 years. Here is a short passage from, "Open The Frontiers-Conversations with Cardinal Suenens" an interview by Karl-Heinz Fleckenstein:

"I'm a man of hope because I believe that with each new day God recreates the world. And so, where God is concerned, we must always be ready for the unexpected. Our lives are not governed by impersonal deterministic laws, nor are we wholly at the mercy of the gloomy forecasts of the sociologists. Always and everywhere God is close to us, unpredictable and loving. I'm an optimist because I believe that the Holy Spirit is God's creative spirit. With each new morning he gives those who welcome Him renewed joy and hope. Who would venture to say that God's love and imagination can be exhausted? Hope is a duty, not a luxury. To hope doesn't mean to dream but to trust God."[50]

Prayer

Prayer is the PETITION of the Holy Spirit. It is the how we communicate with the Trinity: Father, Son and Holy Spirit. There are many forms, styles and methods of prayer: formal and informal; speaking, singing, thinking, reading and listening; private and public. There are also many reasons for prayer: petition, asking for something for ourselves or others; repentance for our errors and transgressions; to praise and honor God the Father, Son and Holy Spirit; and thanksgiving for what God has done for us. Regardless of the form, style, method or reason the charism of prayer boils down to establishing an intimate relationship with the Trinity in conversation - speaking and listening. The Catechism tells us this about prayer:

"In the New Covenant, prayer is the living relationship of the children of God with their Father who is good beyond measure, with his Son Jesus Christ, and with the Holy Spirit. The grace of the Kingdom is 'the union of the entire holy and royal Trinity...with the whole human spirit.'[28] Thus, the life of prayer is the habit of being in the presence of the thrice-holy God and in communion with him. This communion of life is always possible because, through

Baptism, we have already been united with Christ.[29] Prayer is *Christian* insofar as it is communion with Christ and extends throughout the Church, which is his Body. Its dimensions are those of Christ's love."[30] CCC 2565

The charism of prayer gives us insight into what should be prayer's content, our attitude and the ability to "stick with it," to pray for extended periods of time. Here are some examples from scripture, the first is from Jesus' teaching on prayer where He tells the parable about the person who needed bread for his visitors and his neighbor would not get out of bed to give it to him and the need for persistence. The second is the ability to pray for long periods of time like Jesus did, especially, before making important decisions. The third is the ability to accept God's will for us as Jesus did as He prayed to the Father before His crucifixion.

"I tell you, if he does not get up to give him the loaves because of their friendship, he will get up to give him what ever he wants because of his persistence." Luke 11:8

"In those days he departed to the mountain to pray, and he spent the night in prayer to God. When day came, he called his disciples to himself, and from them he chose twelve, whom he also named apostles." Luke 6:12-13

"He advanced a little and fell prostrate in prayer, saying, 'My Father, if it is possible, let this cup pass from me; yet, not as I will, but as you will.'" Matthew 26:39

A form of Charismatic prayer is called "Praying in the Spirit". St. Paul refers to this type of prayer as "praying in tongues". Some find this prayer repulsive and reject it without trying to understand. For myself, I have found Praying in the Spirit as most fulfilling. It allows the Spirit in me to say things to the Trinity that my mind could never conceive. It is the Spirit within me speaking to God. It helps me when my impatience wants to take over; it gets me under control. Refer to the Bibliography for books on the subject. Following are three scriptures related to praying in the Spirit.

"In the same way, the Spirit too comes to the aid of our weakness; for we do not know how to pray as we ought, but the Spirit itself intercedes with inexpressible groanings." Romans 8:26

"[For] if I pray in a tongue, my spirit is at prayer but my mind is unproductive." First Corinthians 14:14

"These are the ones who cause divisions; they live on the natural plane, devoid of the Spirit. But you, beloved, build yourselves up in your most holy faith; pray in the holy Spirit." Jude 19-20

Contemplation

Contemplation is the REFLECTION of the Holy Spirit. If one thinks of their objective as union with God, we can think of this union as an Ordinary Union on one end of a continuum and a Mystical Union on the other end. Think of this union as communication with God through prayer. The lower end or Ordinary Union would start with reading a prayer like the Our Father then progressing to saying it from memory, then to meditating on its meaning. Mystical Union is when one becomes completely oblivious of oneself and completely immersed in God without written or memorized prayers. St. Teresa of Avila expresses it in these words, "God literally took possession of my heart." Contemplative Union falls somewhere in the upper percentile of this continuum and is an important part of a Mystical Union. The Catechism gives us this definition and commentary on contemplation:

"Contemplation: A form of wordless prayer in which mind and heart focus on God's greatness and goodness in affective, loving adoration; to look on Jesus and the mysteries of his life with faith and love." Glossary

"Contemplation is a *gaze* of faith, fixed on Jesus. 'I look at him and he looks at me': this is what a certain peasant of Ars in the time of his holy curé used to say while praying before the tabernacle. This focus on Jesus is a renunciation of self. His gaze purifies our heart; the light of the countenance of Jesus illumines the eyes of our heart and teaches us to see everything in the light of his truth and his compassion for all men. Contemplation also turns its gaze on the mysteries of the light of Christ. Thus it learns the 'interior knowledge of our Lord,' the more to love him and follow him."[31] CCC 2715

When I read this commentary on contemplation, the refrain of one of my very favorite hymns, "Lord When You Come", keeps going around and around in my mind:

"O Lord in my eyes you were gazing, kindly smiling, my name you were saying; all I treasured, I have left on the sand there; close to You, I will find other seas."

For most people, Contemplation is very difficult, especially getting started. It is very difficult for one to empty their mind of all thought and to maintain this emptiness for any sustained period of time. Try it. Remove all thought from your mind, if you can, then time yourself on how long it takes before a thought comes into your mind. It is nearly impossible. The saints were no exception, having this very same problem. The Holy Spirit gave them the solution, the gift of Praying in the Spirit, referred to in writings about them as "jubilation." It is the Spirit praying within you. Your mind is cleared of all thought, lets Jesus in with no interference, and allows you to reflect totally on Him.

There are no rules for developing the charism of contemplation. Like all of the other charisms, it is a free gift from the Holy Spirit. You must pray to Him for it and ask how to develop it as part of your spiritual growth. This is a request the Holy Spirit will not refuse.

If you want to draw others to you so you can help them as Jesus did, you must reflect His image. Jesus was like a magnet drawing others to Him. You also need to be a magnet by having these characteristics of Jesus. That is why the Holy Spirit will give you these five Foundation Charisms when you pray and ask Him.

Chapter 7

Enabling Charisms

Introduction

The enabling charisms are discernment, wisdom, knowledge, prophecy, exhortation and boldness. They are often referred to as the "power tools of the Holy Spirit" because they are the means by which we are allowed by God to use His power and to exert the power of the Holy Spirit that Jesus promised us just before His ascension. Luke felt this message was so important that he presented it in both his Gospel and Acts of the Apostles:

> "And [behold] I am sending the promise [Holy Spirit] of my Father upon you; but stay in the city until you are clothed with power from on high." Luke 24:49

> "But you will receive power when the holy Spirit comes upon you, and you will be my witnesses in Jerusalem, throughout Judea and Samaria, and to the ends of the earth." Acts 1:8

The enabling charisms are introduced in scripture by St. Paul and Luke. The passages quoted below present many charisms. I have underlined the enabling charisms for clarity:

> "Since we have gifts that differ according to the grace given to us, let us exercise them: if <u>prophecy</u> , in proportion to the faith; if ministry, in ministering; if one is a teacher, in teaching; if one exhorts, in <u>exhortation</u>; if one contributes, in generosity; if one is over others, with diligence; if one does acts of mercy, with cheerfulness." Romans 12:6-8 Emphasis Added.

"To one is given through the Spirit the expression of wisdom; to another the expression of knowledge according to the same Spirit; to another faith by the same Spirit; to another gifts of healing by the one Spirit; to another mighty deeds; to another prophecy; to another discernment of spirits; to another varieties of tongues; to another interpretation of tongues." First Corinthians 12:8-10 Emphasis Added.

"As they prayed, the place where they were gathered shook, and they were all filled with the holy Spirit and continued to speak the word of God with boldness." Acts 4:31 Emphasis Added.

Note: Varieties of and interpretation of tongues will not be treated as a separate charisms but included in our discussion on prophecy.

It is very important we understand and accept the relationship between NATURAL GIFTS and SUPERNATURAL GIFTS. They need to work in concert for the greatest benefit and for our efforts to be achieved. Father Francis A. Sullivan, S.J. best explains this relationship in his book Charisms And The Charismatic Renewal A Biblical and Theological Study:

"...In every case the gift of grace [charism] will presuppose, build upon, and perfect the natural capacities that are already present. The 'special grace', which is the charism as such, will add some new capacity and a new readiness to undertake the activity for which it is given. Because of this grace - factor , the activity can rightly be described as 'charismatic' . But it will also involve the person's natural gifts and talents....[38]

In chapter ten, we will consider how to achieve this concert of the natural and supernatural gifts so that our efforts will produce the greatest possible results.

Discernment

Discernment is the JUDGEMENT of the Holy Spirit. This charism is considered first because it plays a key role in our correctly interpreting what we see, hear, think or understand about our use of the other enabling charisms.

The word discernment comes from the Greek word *diakrisis,* which means to distinguish, differentiate or see through to the source. To make correct Christian decisions, one needs to be able to know the source of information, good or bad, and be able to distinguish between several different types of good information.

There are two elements of any situation that one must consider in order to make correct decisions based on God's teachings and will for a particular situation:

- We need to know the source of any idea, thought, suggested action, feeling or situation. There are three possible sources: (1) from the spirit of God which is always right and can never be wrong, (2) from the spirit of Satan, the Evil One, which is always wrong and can never be right or (3) from the human spirit which can be either right, wrong or neutral.

- We need to know if the thought or situation is in conformity with God's will for the particular set of circumstances. Discernment is needed to select the best of several possibilities, even though they are all in conformity with the spirit of God.

Here are some suggestions and tips that will help you make decisions so they will be in concert with the "will of God". First, an exhortation from John that explains what we face:

"Beloved, do not trust every spirit but test the spirits to see whether they belong to God, because many false prophets have gone out into the world. This is how you can know the

Spirit of God: every spirit that acknowledges Jesus Christ come in the flesh belongs to God, and every spirit that does not acknowledge Jesus does not belong to God...."
1 John 4:1-3

- Start with prayer to the Holy Spirit and continue in prayer throughout the discernment process. The purpose of this prayer is not to confirm a decision you have already made but to guide you in making a decision. It is most important to have a period of "quiet" to allow the Holy Spirit to speak to you.

- Be sure you understand clearly your objective or goal. It may be necessary that you discern this first. If you do not have an objective or goal that is in the will of God, you can not get an answer from God to your original question.

- Keep in mind that the Devil or Evil One is just that, evil. He is the great deceiver who makes bad things look good and will play to our wants and desires that may not be in God's will.

- Sometimes it is very hard to discern if something is from our own human spirit because our own wants, desires and emotions play a strong role in our thinking. If something is from our own spirit, even if it is good, we need the Holy Spirit to confirm that it is also from God.

- Consult the main sources of our faith; what Jesus and the Church have told us is right or wrong in the Bible and The Catechism of the Catholic Church.

- We need to use our natural talents and skill to prepare us for hearing the Holy Spirit's decision. This will include: gathering and evaluating information, talking to others, comparing possible answers and studying similar situations.

- Consult others who are close to the Lord: friends, confidants, priests, professionals. This person does not need to be one who is likely to agree with you. You need a different point of view.

- Remember that if something is from God, it will be surrounded with His love, peace and tranquility. There will be a certain "quickening" in our spirit and heart that it is from God. Jesus reminds us that only good can come from God:

"What father among you would hand his son a snake when he asks for a fish? Or hand him a scorpion when he asks for an egg? If you then, who are wicked, know how to give good gifts to your children, how much more will the Father in heaven give the holy Spirit to those who ask him?" Luke 11:11-13

Knowledge & Wisdom

Knowledge is the DIAGNOSIS of the Holy Spirit. Wisdom is the PRESCRIPTION of the Holy Spirit. I am treating the charisms of knowledge and wisdom together because there is a very close relationship between them. Usually knowledge is closely followed by the need for wisdom on how to use the acquired knowledge.

- Supernatural knowledge is information revealed to one by the Holy Spirit which they did not learn through the efforts of the natural mind. It is the mind of Christ working through the Spirit to give one insight and understanding into a situation for which one needs a decision or solution.

- Supernatural wisdom tells us how to apply information learned through supernatural knowledge or the natural mind. It is the mind of Christ telling us through the Holy Spirit what to do or how to do it.

How can these two charisms help you solve problems you face in daily life, at: home, school, community, work or parish? Here is a summary of an episode on the Sally Jessy Raphael Show that presented to parents a purely human solution for resolving children's problems with drug abuse, alcohol abuse, teen sex and much more:

The show featured a consultant who was billed as an expert in helping parents discover and solve hard to identify, but undesirable situations in which their children seemed to be involved. He prescribed three techniques for gathering information: (1) use of hidden cameras, (2) ways of searching a child's room for evidence without getting caught, and (3) ways of surveillance of the child's activities outside the home. Even with the correct information, it was very difficult for the parent to confront the child without raising hostility. One mother who hired this consultant was asked about the outcome. She responded that she had found out what her son was up to, but the gap between mother and son exploded and became even more serious. The consultant admitted that this happens in many of the cases he worked on. As with many human solutions, one problem is solved and another is created.

To use the charisms to help understand and solve the problem, the mother might have remembered that her son is also God's child and He wants to help him. God is the only one that knows all the facts and the best way to solve the problem. He is more than willing to share this information through the Holy Spirit and the charisms of supernatural knowledge (what is happening) and wisdom (what to do about it) This mother needs to pray to the Holy Spirit, asking Him for the knowledge and wisdom she needs to effectively solve this problem.

Prophecy

Prophecy is the MESSAGE of the Holy Spirit. Prophecy is the power to speak the mind of God and His message to us so He can influence, direct or console His people. The purpose of prophecy and how it comes about is explained in scripture:

"Judas and Silas, who were themselves prophets, exhorted and strengthened the brothers with many words." Acts 15:32

"Know this first of all, that there is no prophecy of scripture that is a matter of personal interpretation, for no prophecy ever came through human will; but rather human beings moved by the holy Spirit spoke under the influence of God." Second Peter 1:20-21

"Since we have gifts that differ according to the grace given to us, let us exercise them: if prophecy, in proportion to the faith." Romans 12:6

There are two important things that prophecy is not:

• Prophecy is not fortune telling or predicting the future.

• Prophecy is not some new revelation about our faith. The total deposit of our faith has already been revealed by Jesus in Scripture and the Traditions of the Church.

Bruce Yocum in his book, Prophecy - exercising the prophetic gifts of the spirit in the church today[51] outlines four things God does for us through prophecy:

• Encouragement - "revive a person's spirit, strengthen him or give him hope."

74

- Conviction, Admonition, Correction - "reveal to us our sins, so that we can turn away from sin and be freed from its tyranny."

- Inspiration - "not so much with communicating information as with evoking a response."

- Guidance - "to guide them in His ways. Sometime His guidance was very general...at times that guidance was very specific...can apply to important directional questions as well as to specific individual needs."

The gifts of speaking in tongues and interpretation of tongues are a form of prophecy. This is a rather dramatic way for God to get a message across to His people. One speaks a word of prophecy in a language he and others do not understand. A second person is given the gift of understanding the message and speaking it out in his native language so it can be understood by others.

Scripture tells us that there are false prophets in one form or another roaming the world in sheep's clothing waiting for the opportunity to deceive others. This means that prophecies must be discerned as being either true or false. As a refresher, it would be helpful if you review the section in this chapter on discernment. Remember that a word from God will be frank and straight forward but also very gentle and loving.

Exhortation

Exhortation is the PERSUASION of the Holy Spirit. Some synonyms for exhortation are: arouse, stimulate, persuade, urge, encourage. God realized long before there were effective speaking courses that His people needed to express themselves persuasively if they were to help Him carry out His mission. Exhortation gives us the supernatural ability to speak or write persuasively on behalf of God. It is gentle, not bombastic, vociferous or thunderous. We know that Peter did not take the Dale Carnegie Course before he gave his speech at Pentecost, but it was one of the most dynamic and effective speeches ever made in history. Consider the results:

"Those who accepted his message were baptized, and about three thousand persons were added [to the faith] that day." Acts 2:41

Three thousand may not be a huge crowd of people today, but it certainly was in Peter's day. When you read all of Peter's speech, you will literally feel its exhortive power. Imagine what it must have been like to hear him. You will find it in Acts 2:14-40.

Boldness

Boldness is the COURAGE of the Holy Spirit. This is the gift that gives us the courage to speak out for Jesus Christ in a fearless and daring manner. This is the gift that compels one to speak out or act on the behalf of Jesus Christ regardless of the danger one faces. It makes us willing and able to face physical harm and ridicule for the sake of spreading the "Word of God."

The Sanhedrin was a feared tribunal and most people brought before it were either meek with fear or impudent because of the power this tribunal had over them. When Peter and John were brought before it, not because of a crime but because they healed a crippled beggar, the Sanhedrin witnessed an entirely different reaction. Peter and John were civil and showed no fear and spoke with boldness. Acts of the Apostles, chapter four is littered with examples of their boldness. Here are three:

"Observing the boldness of Peter and John and perceiving them to be uneducated, ordinary men, they were amazed, and they recognized them as the companions of Jesus." Acts 4:13

"And now, Lord, take note of their threats, and enable your servants to speak your word with all boldness." Acts 4:29

"As they prayed, the place where they were gathered shook, and they were all filled with the holy Spirit and continued to speak the word of God with boldness." Acts 4:31

Jesus gives us assurance that the Holy Spirit will be with us whenever we are under attack so we can act with boldness in talking about Him:

"But beware of people, for they will hand you over to courts and scourge you in their synagogues, and you will be led before governors and kings for my sake as a witness before them and the pagans. When they hand you over, do not worry about how you are to speak or what you are to say. You will be given at that moment what you are to say. For it will not be you who speak but the Spirit of your Father speaking through you." Matthew 10:17-20

This is a heavy chapter with much to be understood and accepted. But just think, God wants to share His power with us so that we can continue the work of His Son to make this a better world for you, your family and all God's children. What a privilege!

Chapter 8

Serving Charisms

Introduction

The serving charisms are action oriented. They relate to what one does, or should do, to carry out the role assigned them by Jesus to spread the "Good News" at home, school, parish, community or government. The serving charisms all have a natural counterpart. So, again, it is important for us to remind ourselves that one's natural and supernatural gifts must work in concert if we are going to experience optimum results from our efforts. Remember, God knows all things and is all wise. He is willing to share with us, through the Holy Spirit, information that is not available to one through their natural mind, skills and talents. We need to be docile to the Holy Spirit's prompting.

Keep in mind that a practicing Christian can have more than one serving charism and most do. For example, the principal of a Catholic School could need the charisms of administration, leadership, pastoring and teaching. The Holy Spirit will help you understand the serving charisms you need in your role in life and the specific mission Jesus has given you.

Some people have been particularly gifted by the Spirit in a specific Enabling Charism and are very gifted in helping others in that area. For example, a person so gifted in discernment could have a ministry of discernment to help others. It is a Serving Charism for that person.

Administration

A person who can plan and organize resources to achieve short and long term goals. Responsible for planning, assigning

78

resources, evaluating progress, follow-up, and making adjustments as needed. Must understand clearly the vision and goals of the church, parish, and organization(s) involved and cooperate with and assist leadership of the group. Needs to have exceptional human relations skills. This passage from Daniel speaks of the moral character of a Christian administrator:

"Therefore the supervisors and satraps [governors] tried to find grounds for accusation against Daniel as regards the administration. But they could accuse him of no wrongdoing; because he was trustworthy, no fault of neglect or misconduct was to be found in him." Daniel 6:5

Apostles

A person who adheres to the teachings and life-style of Jesus, a Shepherd and Teacher. Spends all their effort in overseeing others who are responsible for spreading the "Good News" of Jesus. They are direct line successors from the original twelve apostles referred to as "apostolic succession." In the Catholic Church, they are the Bishops of the Church. The Catechism tells us:

"'In order that the full and living Gospel might always be preserved in the Church the apostles left bishops as their successors. They gave them "their own position of teaching authority.'"[32] Indeed, 'the apostolic preaching, which is expressed in a special way in the inspired books, was to be preserved in a continuous line of succession until the end of time.'"[33] CCC 77

Evangelist

Evangelist comes from the Greek word *euangelistos* which means "one who announces the Good News". This is a charism that every Catholic Christian has because of their baptism and confirmation. They are bound, in some way, to pass on the "Good News" they have received to others. Evangelization is a very broad and diverse function of the Church ranging from a simple Christian attitude to complicated apologetic. The Holy Spirit is needed to help discern one's niche in this ministry. Both Paul VI and John Paul II remind us that Holy Spirit is the real evangelizer:

"Evangelization will never be possible without the action of the Holy Spirit."[52]

"The Holy Spirit is indeed the principle agent of the whole of the Church's mission."[53]

Giving

As a member of a Christian Church we are all bound in conscience to tithe from our resources. The charism of giving goes beyond what is required of us, giving until it really hurts and deprives us in some way. An important attitude of someone with this charism is they give willingly and cheerfully. Here is what Jesus has to say about this kind of giver. He refers to the poor widow who put two small coins in the treasury:

"...Amen, I say to you, this poor widow put in more than all the other contributors to the treasury. For they have all contributed from their surplus wealth, but she, from her poverty, has contributed all she had, her whole livelihood." Mark 12:43-44

Healing

It is true of all charisms, especially healing, that the person with the gift is only the conduit through which the Holy Spirit works and manifests His power. To understand this charism, one must realize that Jesus knows what is best for us and that is what He will do, even if it is not the healing we ask for. Most often we think of healing as it refers to our physical health. But what is also very important to our relationship with God is mental and spiritual healing. Jesus may know that one of these is best and will bring one closer to Him. It may also be better for one's spiritual growth if they join Jesus on the cross and learn to suffer with Him. The purpose of healing is to restore one to the fullness of life with Jesus by restoring the body, spirit or mind. The Catechism tells us this about the gift of healing and St. Paul's acceptance of not being healed:

"The Holy Spirit gives to some a special charism of healing [34] so as to make manifest the power of the grace of the risen Lord. But even the most intense prayers do not always obtain the healing of all illnesses. Thus St. Paul must learn from the Lord that 'my grace is sufficient for you, for my power is made perfect in weakness,' and that the sufferings to be endured can mean that 'in my flesh I complete what is lacking in Christ's afflictions for the sake of his Body, that is, the Church.'"[35] CCC 1508

Helper

A person with this charism will do anything, regardless of how menial, to assist others, especially those in leadership, to help them achieve the mission of the Church. They do not look for attention or recognition. The women from Galilee who followed Jesus had the charism of helper to assist Jesus and the Apostles in their mission:

"...and some women who had been cured of evil spirits and infirmities, Mary, called Magdalene, from whom seven demons had gone out, Joanna, the wife of Herod's steward Chuza, Susanna, and many others who provided for them out of their resources." Luke 8:2-3

Leadership

Leadership requires a person who is a visionary, can see how the group should be one, two, three or even 10 years in the future and communicate this to members of the group. It allows a person to organize a team that has a similar vision and the needed skills to reach this vision, One who has this charism helps the group set challenging but attainable goals and motivates them to attain these goals. Above all, in any group, but especially a church group, a leader must be known as a shepherd, a person who is at the service of the group. Jesus is by far the best and most effective model for this style of leadership:

"I am the good shepherd. A good shepherd lays down his life for the sheep. A hired man, who is not a shepherd and whose sheep are not his own, sees a wolf coming and leaves the sheep and runs away, and the wolf catches and scatters them. This is because he works for pay and has no concern for the sheep. I am the good shepherd, and I know mine and mine know me, just as the Father knows me and I know the Father; and I will lay down my life for the sheep." John 10:11-15

Mercy

Mercy is characterized by above average compassion, empathy and kindness to others. However, genuine mercy goes deeper than these feelings, as it involves acts of mercy that comfort and aid others. First, we must look to Jesus as our supreme model of charismatic mercy. In fact, his Divine Mercy requires that we be merciful as explained by Pope John Paul II in his Encyclical, Rich In Mercy.

"Jesus Christ taught that man not only receives and experiences the mercy of God, but that he is also called to practice mercy towards others....In this sense, Christ crucified is for us the loftiest model, inspiration and encouragement. When we base ourselves on this disquieting model, we are able with all humility to show mercy to others."[54]

John Paul, using the parable of the Prodigal Son as an example, points out that forgiveness is a needed prelude to being able to show mercy: It is next to impossible to show Christian mercy toward one with whom we have ill feelings and unforgiveness in our heart. In conclusion, this is what Jesus tells us in the Beatitudes about receiving His Mercy:

"Blessed are the merciful,
    for they will be shown mercy." Matthew 5:7

Ministries

This charism involves a broad range of services to the Church and the Body of Christ: Eucharistic Ministers, Lectors, Sacristans, Ushers, RCIA Sponsors, Choir Member, Catechist, Pre-Marriage, Prison Outreach plus others. Those in these ministries who rely primarily on their own natural talents will not be as successful as those who put their trust in the hands of the Holy Spirit who will put Christ in the center of their ministry. Paul tells us about the esteem he has for those who have a ministry in the Church:

"I urge you, brothers-you know that the household of Stephanas is the firstfruits of Achaia and that they have devoted themselves to the service [ministry] of the holy ones-be subordinate to such people and to everyone who works and toils with them." First Corinthians 16:15-16

Miracles

A miracle occurs when a law of nature has been altered by the supernatural, when an extraordinary event takes place that cannot be explained by the natural. They are sometimes referred to as "signs and wonders". Healing is a form of miracle. The bible records in detail 35 miracles by Jesus of which 25 were healing of the body, mind or spirit. Other miracles dealt with events like turning water to wine, walking on water, the catch of fish, etc. Did Jesus pass on this charism of miracles? Here is what Luke tells us:

"Many signs and wonders were done among the people at the hands of the apostles....Thus they even carried the sick out into the streets and laid them on cots and mats so that when Peter came by, at least his shadow might fall on one or another of them." Acts 5:12, 15

We know that miracles continue in the Church today because this is a requirement for being declared a saint and declaring saints has not ceased. We know that at places like Fatima there are many verified miracles. There are many "everyday miracles," which happen in our everyday life and cannot explained naturally. Often, we pass these miracles off as chance or luck.

Pastor/Pastoring

The Greek word *poimen* can be translated as either shepherd or pastor. Jesus was never referred to as pastor, but always as a Shepherd and sometimes as the "Good Shepherd." Jesus understood the importance of such an office to care for the spiritual needs of His Church if it were to grow. He set up a hierarchy of Pope, the Chief Shepherd, Bishops, and Priests. One of their prime functions is administration of the Sacraments. Today the word pastor is more often used than shepherd, but the meaning is the same. Pastors have a flock to watch over, protect and guide. There is also a function of pastoring that is exercised by lay people. They can have the responsibility, under the Pastor, of shepherding a sub-group within the Church; watch over, protect and guide. They do not have any authority to administer Sacraments except in ways they can assist the Pastor as designated by the Church.

"For you had gone astray like sheep, but you have now returned to the shepherd and guardian of your souls."
1 Peter 2:25

Teacher

The Magisterium of the Church (Pope and Bishops) is its official teaching body. Of course, the charism of teaching is needed throughout the Church by anyone in a position to pass on information to others: theologians, pastors, school teachers, religion teachers and parents. The list goes on and on. The charism of teaching helps primarily in three ways: it gives the teacher a good and truthful understanding of the subject, it gives the teacher insights into how best to present the subject, and it gives a personality that attracts others to listen and believe, a Christian Model. These characteristics are most needed when the subject is the Catholic Faith or in a Catholic School, but they will also be helpful to make one an effective teacher in a public situation. St. James was well aware of the importance of teaching. He referred to it as the "Power of the Tongue" and compared it to the bit in a horse's mouth, a small rudder on a ship, and how a small fire can set a huge blaze. It is not St. Jame's purpose to discourage teaching vocations. He does want them to understand the power they have to influence others and use it wisely:

"Not many of you should become teachers, my brothers, for you realize that we will be judged more strictly...."
James 3:1

This concludes our presentation on the charims - the gifts of the Holy Spirit. They give us the power Jesus promised us to deal with the evil in the world and make it a better place for us to live. Luke 10:19 tells us, "Behold, I have given you the power 'to tread upon serpents' and scorpions and upon the full force of the enemy and nothing will harm you." This enemy is Satan and only the supernatural power of the Holy Spirit is capable of conquering him. The Charisms help us become more like Jesus which gives us the power that Jesus had to conquer Satan and gives each of us a special mission to serve Him.

Chapter 9

Your Christian Growth

Introduction

The purpose of this chapter is to help you in your Christian Growth, especially its charismatic dimension. Here are six thought starter messages for you to read and meditate on. Do so with periods of silence so the Holy Spirit has an opportunity speak to you. Regardless of your level of growth as a Christian these meditations can help you move to a higher level.

Stages of Growth

Let's look at a model based on the development of a butterfly as presented by Father John Hampsch, CMF Director of Claretian Ministry. He made this presentation at the Silverdome in Pontiac, MI, July 30, 1988. He used the image of a butterfly's development because its growth process is very similar to what we as Christians should go through: start as an egg, grow into a caterpillar, then a cocoon, and finally a butterfly. This process is called metamorphosis, which means a marked change in appearance, character and function. This should happen to each of us in our growth as a Christian.

Egg Stage: This is the Sacramental Stage when we are initiated into the Christian life through Baptism, Confirmation and Eucharist. The Church uses this term, neophyte, as the designation for one who has gone through a period of instruction and received the Sacraments of Baptism, Confirmation and Eucharist. They are now a "New Person."

Caterpillar Stage: This is the Evangelized Stage when one starts to look beyond the rules, regulations, dogmas learned in the

Egg Stage. We have a "metanoia", which means a "change of thinking" not only in our minds but even more importantly in our hearts. This brings about a change in our lifestyle and values. We see Jesus Christ as the Lord of our life, put Him in charge, and form a very personal relationship with Him. We stop sinning not because it is a rule of the Church but because it offends and hurts Jesus Christ who died on the cross for us.

Cocoon Stage: This is the Charismatic Stage when we realize the importance of the gift of the Holy Spirit from the Father and Son. We realize our privilege in using God's power through the charisms of the Holy Spirit. This stage completes confirmation by activating the Power of the Holy Spirit received in this sacrament and motivates us to action. It is characterized by a continuing Pentecost experience in our life.

Butterfly Stage: This is the Contemplative or Mystical Stage. One does not lose what they gained in the other stages but is moved to a higher level and an extremely close union with God; Father, Son and Holy Spirit. One receives a very personal revelation from God, about this relationship and what He expects. Father Hampsch says we are a "rose bud becoming a rose."

Where do you fit in this model? With most people there is no clear line of demarcation between each stage. Often there is an overlap. The goal of this book is to help you and the Church become solidly fixed in the Cocoon Stage of Christian Growth. You have experienced the *Upper Room* and a New Pentecost.

God's Love

If we are going to grow as a Christian, it is important that we not just know about God's love but also recognize and experience it. We must accept His love without question regardless of what evil we have done or how low we think of ourselves. It is then we will feel His love strongly enough to pass it on to others as Jesus commands us.

"I have told you this so that my joy may be in you and your joy may be complete. This is my commandment: love one another as I love you. No one has greater love than this, to lay down one's life for one's friends."
John 15:11-13

Is Jesus the love of your life? Are you a model of His love? Can you pass it on to others who do not know Him?

Salvation

The Father sent us His Son, Jesus, to suffer, die on the cross and be resurrected from the dead for our salvation:

"But God proves his love for us in that while we were still sinners Christ died for us....Indeed, if, while we were enemies, we were reconciled to God through the death of his Son, how much more, once reconciled, will we be saved by his life." Romans 5:8, 10

Our salvation involves three periods of time: past, present and future, as pointed out in the following scriptures:

A Historical Reality - I have been saved.

"He saved us and called us to a holy life, not according to our works but according to his own design and the grace bestowed on us in Christ Jesus before time began."
Second Timothy 1:9

An Ongoing Experience - I am being saved.

"All of us, gazing with unveiled face on the glory of the Lord, are being transformed into the same image from glory to glory, as from the Lord who is the Spirit."
Second Corinthians 3:18

88

A Future Event - I will be saved.

"We know that all creation is groaning in labor pains even until now; and not only that, but we ourselves, who have the firstfruits of the Spirit, we also groan within ourselves as we wait for adoption, the redemption of our bodies." Romans 8:22-23

Are you cooperating with God in His plan for your salvation? He does not need your help but wants it.

New Life In Jesus

Imagine the anguish, it is late July and you are returning from a two week vacation. You rush out the back door to take a look at your tomato plants, which were doing very well when you left. Now they are very wilted and their yellow blossoms hardly detectable. Your heart sinking you think water will not help but it is worth a try. So, you get a watering can of fresh water from the water purifier assuring nothing will contaminate the plants. You give each of the plants a good healthy drink and then go about unloading the car. When you check the plants about an hour later, they have regained most of their healthy look. A second watering brings them completely back to life. Jesus knows the value of "living water" as He explained to the Samaritan woman at Jacob's well about "living water:"

"'...Everyone who drinks this water will be thirsty again; but who ever drinks the water I shall give will never thirst; the water I shall give will become in him a spring of water welling up to eternal life." John 4:13-14

"A thief comes only to steal and slaughter and destroy; I come so that they might have a life and have it more abundantly." John 10:10

Is Jesus Christ the Lord of your life or is something else between you and His offer of a "New Life" with Him?

Forgiveness

To forgive someone who has hurt you is not easy. Jesus knows this because of what was done to Him on the cross, but He did forgive them.

"Then Jesus said, 'Father, forgive them, they know not what they do.'..." Luke 23:34

Jesus also tells us how important forgiveness is to our own salvation:

"If you forgive others their transgressions, your heavenly Father will forgive you. But if you do not forgive others, neither will your Father forgive your transgressions." Matthew 6:14-15

"Then Peter approaching asked him, 'Lord, if my brother sins against me, how often must I forgive him? As many as seven times?' Jesus answered, 'I say to you, not seven times but seventy-seven times.'" Matthew 18:21-22

This is a big order but a better understanding of forgiveness and what is expected will help:

- Our salvation depends on forgiving others. Also, our capacity to have the Holy Spirit in us and His power available to us might depend on our forgiving others.

- Forgiving is a process, and takes time. It may be we can forgive only a little at a time. Jesus is not as concerned with our success as much as He is with our intentions and efforts.

90

- Forgiveness is an initial act of the will. It is a decision we want to make in the name of Jesus. We will to forgive even though our emotions may tell us we cannot.

- Memories of a wrong done to us will linger. We need the counsel of the Holy Spirit to help us effectively deal with these memories.

Do you appreciate that if you do not forgive you are a slave? Only forgiveness can set you free.

Spiritual Gifts

We have already covered the spiritual gifts or charisms which represent the power of God offered to us through the Holy Spirit. I suggest that you briefly review chapters six, seven and eight to refresh your memory of the charisms.

Considering your current situation, which of these charisms do you most need to enhance your Christian Growth and make you a more effective disciple of Jesus Christ at home, work, community, school or parish?

A Prayer of Commitment

- " Father, I want Your Son, Jesus Christ, to be Lord of my life. I will put Him in charge of every aspect of my life. You sent Him out of Your great love for me and Your great desire for me to spend eternity with You, Your Son, and the Holy Spirit. I know, without a doubt, that I can trust Jesus with my life because He suffered and died on the cross for me. Amen."

- "I want to live to the fullest Your plan for my life, including the particular mission Jesus has for me. I ask Him to reveal this to me and help me be an image of Him and His love so it will shine in the world for others to see. Amen."

- "Dear Jesus, I forgive from my heart anyone who has wronged me and I ask You to forgive me my offenses against You and any of Your people. I am truly sorry for them. Amen."

- "I know that I cannot do any of this with just my own natural power. I need Your supernatural power which You offer to me through the Holy Spirit. I ask that You give me the spiritual gifts, the charisms, I need to effectively carry out Your plan for my life. Amen."

This is a chapter one should read, study and meditate on over and over again. The Holy Spirit will always reveal new insights and understandings to you so your Christian Growth will always be on an upward spiral and you will live your life in the joy and peace Jesus Christ intends for you.

Plan For My
Christian Growth

Use this page to sketch out some action steps you are going to take that will implement Chapter 9 in your life. Start out by setting a vision of how Christian Growth can and will change your life.

Chapter 10

How to Use The Spirit's Power

Introduction

The last chapter of this book is the most important. You can understand and accept all there is to know about the Charismatic Dimension of the Church, the Holy Spirit and the Spiritual Gifts, but if you do not understand how to turn this knowledge into *action* not much will be gained. The Holy Spirit is a person of *action* and expects us to use His power to act effectively.

The Holy Spirit's Mode of Operation

The Holy Spirit helps us live an exemplary and effective Christian life by acting as:

- Our Advocate (NAB) or (NJB) - John 14:26

- Our Source of Consolation - Acts 9:31

- Our Counselor - Mark 13:11 (NAB) or John 14:26 (RSV)

- Our Informer - Acts 20:22-23

- Our Source of Joy - Acts 13:52

- Our Source of God's Power - Luke 10:19, 24:49; Acts 1:8

- Our Source of Renewal - Titus 3:5

- Our Teacher of Truth - John 14:17

The Holy Spirit's desirable and needed influences on one's life are manifested in four basic ways:

- Through the sacraments, initially Baptism and Confirmation, then the other five sacraments, especially Reconciliation and Eucharist. Much has already been written on this source of the Holy Spirit, so will not be a subject of this book.

- The Holy Spirit acts spontaneously on His own without our specific solicitation to help us out of an undesirable situation we are probably not aware of. Recently I was on Hickory Grove Road, near St. Hugo's School, approaching Opdyke Road an intersection I have passed through thousands of times. I knew that if a car coming south on Opdyke was north of the railroad tracks I had plenty of time to safely enter the intersection and proceed, because this was a four way stop. A red car coming south was still well north of the tracks, so I started into the intersection and instantly heard in my mind the word "STOP", I slammed on my brakes as the red car went sailing through the intersection and stop sign at about 90 miles per hour. I probably would not be here today if it had not been for that message "Stop" from the Holy Spirit.

- One prays to the Holy Spirit asking for His help in a specific situation and the Spirit responds. This could be spontaneous, a prayer card, or a novena much like we would pray to Mary or the saints. One of my favorites is St. Augustine's prayer "Come Holy Spirit Enlighten Me" in which we invoke Him to make us holy in several areas of our life. This approach lacks the action the Holy Spirit expects of us. We are to use His supernatural power to solve a problem or correct a situation. This brings us to the fourth way the Holy Spirit can help us.

- Jesus ordained that we use the supernatural power available to us through the Holy Spirit to carry out the mission He assigned to us depending on our station in life:

"But you will receive power when the holy Spirit comes upon you, and you will be my witnesses in Jerusalem, throughout Judea and Samaria, and to the ends of the earth." Acts 1:8

It is important to keep in mind that Jesus is not just talking about evangelization in a technical sense but in every way we conduct our life. For example, the way we raise our family or the way a Worship Commission meeting is conducted. He expects us to use the Foundation, Enabling, and Serving Charisms to do our part in solving problems and correcting undesirable situations. We should not simply depend on our natural abilities or for "someone upstairs" to take care of it for us. We are to use these supernatural gifts in concert with our natural gifts. This is especially true of the six Enabling charisms talked about in Chapter 7: Discernment, Knowledge, Wisdom, Prophecy, Exhortation and Boldness.

The fourth way the Holy Spirit works in our lives is what this book is all about, using the charims to put Holy Spirit Power into our thinking and actions.

Need For Docility

A key factor in the Holy Spirit's ability to help us is our docility to Him. The dictionary defines docile as being ready and willing to be taught or teachable. The two greatest and most important examples of docility to the Holy Spirit since the beginning of time are: (1) The Virgin Mary's acceptance of her pregnancy by the power of the Holy Spirit bringing us The Word Incarnate, Jesus Christ, Luke 1:26-38, the story of Jesus' birth and (2) St. Joseph's acceptance of Mary into his home as his wife and his role as Foster Father of Jesus, Matthew 1:18-25. A more current example of docility to the Spirit was that of Blessed Pope John XXIII which moved the Church in a direction of growth. Léon Joseph Cardinal Suenens. a dear and close confidant to Pope John and a Moderator of Vatican II, observed that the greatest attribute of the Pope was his docility and his willingness to be taught by the Spirit.

Docility is one's first step in allowing the Holy Spirit to be your guide through life. Become docile to Him and let Him teach you. Discernment is another attribute that I believe Mary, Joseph and Pope John had. They were sure that the message they received was from the Spirit of God, and not from themselves or Satan.

The key to docility is three fold: be quiet, be patient and listen.

A Prayer To The Holy Spirit

If we expect the Holy Spirit to do all the things for us that have been summarized in this chapter, we must commit ourselves to Him and pray to Him daily. Here is a "Morning Prayer To The Holy Spirit" we should start with every day:

"Blessed Trinity, Father, Son and Holy Spirit: I thank you for bringing me to this new day and giving me an opportunity to be of service to Your Church and Your people here on earth. I ask You to be with me in everything I do, think or say so all that I do, think or say is according to Your will for me. Amen."

"I ask You, Jesus, to protect me and my loved ones with Your Precious Blood so that the Evil One cannot come against us. Help me become docile to the Holy Spirit as Mary and Joseph were to bring us the 'Word Incarnate.' Jesus Christ. Amen."

"Holy Spirit, I ask you to strengthen in me the Foundation Charisms. Increase in me the ability to _pray_, to communicate with the Trinity. Help me to put all my _faith_ and trust in Jesus who saved me, a sinner. Let this bring me true Christian _hope_ that will characterize me and give hope to others. Help me to accept You as Lord of my life and

Your *love* for me so this *love* will shine through me to others. Help me have *contemplative* moments when I am very near to Jesus and can feel His very presence. Amen."

"Holy Spirit, help me be true and faithful to my station in life: married, single, parent. Remind me of the Serving Charisms you have assigned to me and help me carry them out effectively and faithfully according to Your plan for me. Amen."

"Holy Spirit, I ask that the power of God, which Jesus promised to each of us through the Spirit's Enabling Charisms work in concert with my natural gifts, also from God. Help me use these charisms to solve the problems and undesirable situations in my life at home, community, school, government, work, and parish. I have a particular need to resolve the following: _____. Amen."

"Holy Spirit strengthen me with Your supernatural gifts of discernment, knowledge, wisdom, prophecy, exhortation, and boldness so that my decisions and actions are made with the help of their power. That they are made according to God's divine plan for my life and others involved and will lead us closer to you. Amen."

" Holy Spirit I thank and praise You from my heart for the help I have already received, especially: _____. Amen."

Keep Your Eyes On The Spirit

It is not only necessary to start your day in the Power of the Holy Spirit but to come to Him during the day, especially at times of particular need. It can be as simple as:

"Holy Spirit, please help me. I need Your power right now to solve this situation _____. Amen."

Or, it can be a little longer and more specific as:

> "Holy Spirit, I need Your help regarding (state your need or situation you are dealing with). Please give me the gift(s) of discernment, knowledge and wisdom I need to strengthen my natural skills and talents so I can make a decision or take an action reflecting the divine will of God that resolves the situation." Amen

Prayer Principles

These sample prayers demonstrate four principles one should follow when asking the Holy Spirit for help:

- The prayer is addressed directly to the Holy Spirit.

- The prayer states a situation that needs attention.

- The prayer states that you intend to use *your efforts* with the help of the Holy Spirit to solve the situation.

- It indicates you need the Spirit's supernatural power to work in concert with your natural skills and talents.

How About Organizations?

Using the power of the Holy Spirit in groups or organizations is more difficult. It is possible some members have a lack of understanding about the Spirit's ways or may not accept the Charismatic Dimension of the Church. Relying on the Spirit must start with leadership and their willingness to be patient and guide the membership. Those in the group who believe in the power of the Holy Spirit and how it can be used must pray silently before and during the meeting that the Power of the Spirit will prevail.

Here are several suggestions for motivating a group to depend on the power of the Spirit through His supernatural gifts at least as much as they depend on their own natural skills and talents to make decisions:

- Father Raniero Contalamessa, O.F.M.,Cap. former preacher to the Vatican household reminded us in his book, The Holy Spirit in the Life of Jesus,[55] that Jesus always prayed at length before making a decision. He tells us that "the greater the time devoted to prayer over some problem, the less time will be needed in solving it."

- If we expect the Holy Spirit to help we must give Him time to talk. The formula should be: pray to Him, be silent and listen for His response, make your decision, and then act..

- It is certainly important to open and close a meeting with a prayer. Equally important during the meeting is to pause briefly before an important decision is to be made and ask for the Holy Spirit's direction.

- A work group connected with the Church should start their day with a brief prayer dedicating their efforts to God and asking the Holy Spirit for guidance in their work.

This is the end of my book. Thanks for reading it. I trust you found it interesting and educational regarding the Charismatic Dimension of the Church. I hope and pray it will motivate you to accept the Power of the Holy Spirit to make your world and the world of others a better place to live in. Please leave me a message on my web site: www.holyspiritpower.org or send me an e-mail: bob@holyspiritpower.org God Bless You.

My Plan For
Using Holy Spirit Power
In my Life

First, set a vision of how you see Holy Spirit Power working in your life. Next, review Chapters 6, 7, and 8 which are about the charisms. Now, turn to page 96 and pray the Prayer To The Holy Spirit asking for guidance in this venture that will bring you closer to Jesus Christ and the peace and love He promises.

Thoughts on the Holy Spirit by Early Church Writers

Ignatius of Antioch: (died 107 AD)

This Bishop of Antioch, Syria pointed out in his writing that he had the gifts of *prophecy, word of knowledge* and *word of wisdom.* The Holy Spirit would speak to him, especially when he was preaching or teaching.

Justin Martyr: (100-165 AD)

A layperson, author, teacher and theologian who wrote two books titled A*pologies.* In his book *Dialogue with Trypho,* he referred to Christian initiation as Baptism in the Spirit and related it to Jesus' baptism in the Jordan.

Tertullian: (160-225 AD)

A lay theologian and moralist who was concerned that the Holy Spirit could be locked up in a book (the bible) and not available for daily guidance of the people. There was some truth in this because for years the Holy Spirit was often referred to as "the lost person of the Trinity". Whenever speaking or writing about the gifts of the Holy Spirit, he quoted the Pauline gifts from 1 Corinthians 12.

Hippolytus: (170-236 AD)

He was a theologian who became an anti-pope but reconciled with the Church before his death. In his writing, *Apostolic Tradition,* he wrote extensively about the gifts, charisms, of the Holy Spirit. He stressed that the laity as well as the clergy received and could exercise these gifts. A favorite quote of his was Mark 16:17-18

102

where Jesus promised those who believed in Him that they would perform signs and wonders.

Origen: (185-254 AD)

A theologian who was known for the bible commentaries he wrote. He was considered to have a "vast" knowledge of history and the Church and considered the Holy Spirit as the source of our holiness. He considered prophecy a very important charism and quoted Psalm 81:10b (RSV) as instructions for stimulating this gift. In this verse, God tells us to open our mouths and he will fill them`.

Eusedius of Casearea: (260-340 AD)

He was considered the "Father of Church History" and wrote *The History of the Church.* Often in his writings, he would start out a statement with "...the Holy Spirit says". He wrote a commentary on the Psalms in which he referred to the charisms of wisdom, word of knowledge, faith, healing, and tongues.

Epharem of Syria: (306-373 AD)

A deacon and teacher who became a Doctor of the Church. He wrote considerably on the Holy Spirit. In his *Hymns of Faith,* he wrote about *Fire and Spirit* in: Mary's womb, the Jordan river, our baptism, and the Bread and Cup. He considered our baptism a Pentecost Event.

Cyril of Jerusalem: (310-386 AD)

Cyril was Bishop of Jerusalem and is a Doctor of the Church. He gave many lectures and wrote on Catechesis. At least six times he referred to the charisms, gifts of the Holy Spirit, as presented by Paul in 1 Corinthians 12. He challenged his listeners and readers to be open to the *Heavenly Charisms* given to us by God through the Holy Spirit.

Hilary of Poitiers: 315-368 AD)

He was Bishop of Poitiers and writer. His book on the Trinity, *De Trinitate*, is a classic. He stressed that the gifts of the Holy Spirit as St. Paul wrote about are still valid today. This bothered him because as the Church became more established the charisms had started to disappear. He often gave the image of the Holy Spirit as *Rain-Creeks-Mighty Rivers*. His tract on the Psalm pointed out the gifts of the Holy Spirit.

Gregory of Nazianzus: (329-389 AD)

He was a monk, scholar, writer, and theologian. He was known for his *Theological Addresses On The Holy Spirit* and *Orations On Pentecost*. He claimed one can receive the charisms before baptism (he gives Cornelius in Acts as an example) but that at baptism is the normal time to receive the charisms.

Basil of Caesarea: (330-379 AD)

A presbyter or priest and theologian. He was the channel of many miraculous healings. His writings on the Holy Spirit were so voluminous, including *On The Holy Spirit*, that he was called *Doctor of the Holy Spirit*. He placed receiving of the charisms in the context of Christian Initiation.

Gregory of Nyssa: (330-395 AD)

He was Bishop of Nyssa, a theologian, and a prodigy. The charisms were beginning to wane, so he spoke out on this often, pointing out they were important to the Church and must be present in the Church.. He often spoke of the Spirit as the *Breath of God*.

Some Helpful Prayers

Prayer to the Holy Spirit by St. Augustine

Breath in me
O Holy Spirit,
That my thoughts
May all be *Holy*

Act In me,
O Holy Spirit
That my work, too,
May be *Holy.*

Draw my heart,
O Holy Spirit,
That I love
But what is *Holy.*

Strengthen me,
O Holy Spirit,
To defend
All that is *Holy,*

Guard me then,
O Holy Spirit,
That I always
May be *Holy.*

Prayer to the Holy Spirit by Cardinal Mercier

Holy Spirit, beloved of my soul,
I adore you.

Enlighten me, guide me,
strengthen me, console me.

Tell me what I should do,
give me Your orders.

I promise to submit myself
to all that You desire of me
and to accept all that You
permit to happen to me.

Let me only know Your will.

Prayer for healing by Bob Williams

Heavenly Father in the name of Your Son, Jesus,
and the Holy Spirit, touch and anoint me, and help me
receive Your love and peace. Grant me who seeks
to be restored to the fullness of life in You, the physical,
mental, and spiritual healing I need. Holy Spirit give me
the charism of faith to believe that whatever I ask for in
prayer with trust I will receive from You. Amen

Notes

Cf. means confer or compare to

1. Petition in the Our Father "But deliver us from evil."

2. John 8:44; Revelation 12:9.

3. Council of Trent, (1546): DS 1511; Cf. Hebrews 2:14.

4. Cf. Genesis 3:1-5; Wisdom 2:24.

5. Cf. John 8:44; Revelation 12:9.

6. Cf. Mark 1:12-13.

7. Luke 4:13.

8. Cf. Dogmatic Constitution on the Church 12.

9. Cf. 1 Corinthians 12.

10. Council of Constantinople II (553): DS 421.

11. Council of Toledo XI (675): DS 530:26

12. Fides Damasi: DS 71.

13. Council of Toledo XI (675): DS 530:25

14. Lateran Council IV (1215): DS 804.

15. Cf. Sacrosantum Concilium 6, Dogmatic Constitution on the Church 2

16. 1 Corinthians 11:26.

17. Cf. 1 Corinthians 13.

18. Cf. John 4:14 & 7:38-39.

19. *Epiciesis* means invocation upon the gifts - bread & wine

20. Cf. Roman Missal, EP I (Roman Canon) 90.

21. Galatians 5:22-23.

22. Galatians 5:25; Cf. Matthew 16:24-26

23. Cf. Dogmatic Constitution on the Church 12.

24. Cf.1 Corinthians 12.

25. Dei Verbum 5; Cf. Denzinger-Schonmetzer, Enchiridion Symbolorum 377; 3010.

26. Hebrews 10:23

27. Titus 3:6-7.

28. St. Gregory of Nazianzus, *Oratio* 16, 9: PG 35, 945.

29. Cf. Romans 6:5.

30. Cf. Ephesians 3:18-21

31. Cf.St. Ignatius of Loyola, *Spiritual Exercises* , 104.

32. Dei Verbum 7:2; St.Irenaeus, *Adv. haeres.* 3,3, 1:PG 7, 848; Harvey, 2,9.

33. Dei Verbum 8:1

34. Cf.1 Corinthians 12:9,28,30.

108

35. 2 Corinthians 12:9; Colossians 1:24

36. Pope John Paul II, Mission of the Redeemer - Encyclical, (Boston, St. Paul Books & Media), 9

37. Austin Flannery, Vatican Council II, Volume I-Concliar and Post Canciliar Documents, Rev. Ed. (Newport, NY; Costello, 1996) 363-4

38. Francis A. Sullivan, Charisms and Charismatic Renewal - A Biblical and Theological Study, (Ann Arbor, Servant, 1982) 13

39. Pope John Paul II, The Spirit, Giver of Life and Love - Catechesis on The Creed, (Boston, Pauline Books & Media, 1996) 80

40. Jurgrens, The Fathers of the Early Church, Vol. 1, (Collegeville, MN, Liturgical Press, 1970) 363

41. St Joseph Sunday Missal - Prayerbook and Hymnal, (NJ, Catholic Book, 1999) 33

42. William R. Farmer, The International Bible Commentary, (Collegeville, MN, Liturgical Press, 1998) 1295

43. Michael Scanlan & James Manney, Let the Fire Fall 2nd ed, (Stubenville, OH, Franciscan, 1997) 96

44. Austin Flannery, Vatican Council I - The Conciliar and Post Conciliar Documents Rev. Ed., (Newport, NY, Costello, 1982) 363-4

45. Kilian McDonnell & George T. Montague, Christian Initiation and Baptism in the Spirit - Evidence from the First Eight Centuries, Rev. Ed., (Collegeville, MN, Liturgical Press 1994) Precis, 40, 89, 90, 342, 343, 357, 371.

109

46. Pope John XXIII, Journal Of A Soul, (NYC, Image Doubleday, 1980) 326

47. Walter M Abbott, The Documents of Vatican II, Vol. 1 (American Press, 1966) 709

48. Austin Flannery, Vatican Council II, Volume 1 - The Conciliar and Post Conciliar Documents, Rev. Ed., (Newport, NY, Costello, 1996) 769

49. Austin Flannery, Vatican Council II, Vol, 1 - The Conciliar and Post Conciliar Documents, Rev. Ed, (Newport, NY, Costello, 1996) 880

50. Karl-Heinz Fleckenstein, Open the Frontiers - Conversations with Cardinal Suenens, NYC, Seabury, 1981

51. Bruce Yocum, Prophecy, (Ann Arbor, Servant, 1976) 39-40, 42-43

52. Pope Paul VI, Evangelization In the Modern World, (Washington, D.C., U,S. Catholic Conference, 1975) 55

53. Pope John Paul II, Mission of the Redeemer - Encyclical, (Boston, St. Paul Books & Media) 33

54. Pope John Paul II, Rich In Mercy, Encyclical, (Washington, D.C., U.S. Catholic Conference, 1981) 45

55. Raniero Cantalamessa, The Holy Spirit in the Life of Jesus - The Mystery of Christ's Baptism, (Collegeville, MN, Liturgical Press) 63

56. Léon Joseph Cardinal Suenens, A New Pentecost? (New York, The Seabury Press, 1957) Hardback 7, Paperback 18

Bibliography

Cantalamessa, Fr. Raniero. *The Holy Spirit in the Life of Jesus - The Mystery of Christ's Baptism*: The Liturgical Press, 1994

DeArteaga, William, *Quenching The Spirit - Discover the Real Spirit Behind the Charismatic Controversy*: Creation House, Strong Communications, Co., 1996

Fortuna, Fr. Stan C.F.R.. *U GOT 2 BELIEVE*: Our Sunday Visitor Publishing Division, Inc, 2001

Ghezzi, Bert, *Miracles of the Saints - True Stories of Lives Touched by the Supernatural*: Zendervan Publishing House, 1996

Hampsch, John H. C.M.F., *The Gift of Tongues (tape)*, and *Why You Should Pray In Tongues*, Claretian Tape Ministry,

Lang, J. Stephen, *1,001 Things You Always Wanted to Know About the Holy Spirit*: Thomas Nelson Publisher, 1999

McBride, Fr. Alfred, *The Gospel of the Holy Spiri - Meditations and Commentary on the Acts of the Apostles*: Our Sunday Vustor Publishing Division, 1992

McDonnell, Fr. Kilian and Montague, Fr. George T., *Christian Initiation and Baptism in the Holy Spirit - Evidence from The First Eight Centuries; Second, Revised Edition*: The Litugical Press, 1994

Montagure. Fr. George T., *Still Riding the Wind - Learning the Ways of the Spirit*: Resurrection Press, 1984

Paul, Pope John II, *The Spirit, Giver of Life and Love*: Pauline Books & Media, 1996

Ranaghan, Deacon Kevin M., *In The Power Of The Spirit - Effective Catholic Evangelization*: Resurrection Press, 1991

Scanlan, Fr. Michael with Manney, James, *Let the Fire Fall*: Franciscan University Press, 1997

Scanlan, Fr. Michael with Manney, James, *What Does God Want? A Practical Guide to Making Decision*: Our Sunday Visitor Publishing Division, 1996

Schreck, Alan, *Hearts Aflame - The Holy Spirit at the Heart of Christian Living Today*: Servent Publications, 1995

Suenens, Cardinal Léon Joseph, *A New Pentecost?*: The Seabury Press, 1975; Out of print, worth hunting for used copy

Walsh, Msgr. Vincent M., *The Spirit of Jesus*: Key of David Publications, 1984

Upcoming Books
By The Author

- **The Basic Of Evangelization For Individuals-
  How To Be Part Of Jesus' Mission**

- **Setting Up A Parish For Effective Evangelization-
  Let the Holy Spirit Be Your Guide**

- **Why I Believe In The Real Presence-
  Jesus Is Really And Truly In the Eucharist**

- **How To Answer the Sola Scriptura Question-
  Capital "T" Tradition Is Needed**

- **The Holy Spirit and Jesus' Mother Mary
  Whata Team!**